New Islamic Schools

New Islamic Schools

Tradition, Modernity, and Class in Urban Pakistan

Sanaa Riaz

NEW ISLAMIC SCHOOLS
Copyright © Sanaa Riaz, 2014.

All rights reserved.

First published in 2014 by PALGRAVE MACMILLAN® in the United States—a division of St. Martin's Press LLC, 175 Fifth Avenue, New York, NY 10010.

Where this book is distributed in the UK, Europe and the rest of the world, this is by Palgrave Macmillan, a division of Macmillan Publishers Limited, registered in England, company number 785998, of Houndmills, Basingstoke, Hampshire RG21 6XS.

Palgrave Macmillan is the global academic imprint of the above companies and has companies and representatives throughout the world.

Palgrave® and Macmillan® are registered trademarks in the United States, the United Kingdom, Europe and other countries.

ISBN: 978-1-137-38246-7

Library of Congress Cataloging-in-Publication Data

Riaz, Sanaa.
  New Islamic schools : tradition, modernity, and class in urban Pakistan / Sanaa Riaz.
     pages cm
  Includes bibliographical references and index.
  ISBN 978-1-137-38246-7 (hardcover : alk. paper)
  1. Islamic education—Pakistan. 2. Islamic religious education—Pakistan. I. Title.
  LC910.P3R53 2014
  371.077—dc23
                                                              2013044029

A catalogue record of the book is available from the British Library.

Design by Amnet.

First Edition: May 2014

10 9 8 7 6 5 4 3 2 1

To Razia Riaz, the woman who dreamed dauntlessly,
and Riazuddin, the clever man who let her . . .
To my middle-class heroes, who braved bringing liberalism
home to their daughters . . .

Contents

List of Tables		ix
A Note on Transliteration		xi
Acknowledgments		xiii
1	Introduction: Understanding Tradition, Modernity, and Class in Islamic Education	1
2	Situating the Islamic Schooling Trend in Pakistan	13
3	The Educational System in Pakistan and the Place of Islamic Schooling	49
4	Examining Diversity in Islamic Schools	87
5	Knowledge at Play	113
6	Toward a New Approach to Islamic Education	161
Notes		167
Bibliography		177
Glossary		183
Index		187

List of Tables

Table 1.1	Economic and Social Standing of Islamic Schools and Their Patrons Based on Income-Level Areas	5
Table 3.1	Education Policy: 1998–2010	55
Table 3.2	Review of Subjects Taught in Grades 1–8 in Public Schools, Private Schools, and Madrasas	59
Table 3.3	Review of Subjects Taught in Grades 9 and 10 in Public Schools, Private Schools, and Madrasas	59
Table 3.4	Subjects Taught in Islamic Schools and Their Nature of Inclusion	85

A Note on Transliteration

This book does not use diacritics anywhere for Arabic or Arabic-origin words. I follow the IJMES guide throughout, with the exception of popular usage. In the case of Urdu words, regardless of their origins, I use popular Pakistani English spellings.

Acknowledgments

I can't thank enough my dissertation advisor, Dr. Jerome C. Rose, for standing by me through thick and thin. I sincerely thank Dr. Mary Jo Schneider for patiently and meticulously reading this manuscript in its incipient stages. My sincere thanks to Dr. Dolores L. Burke for reading the work and providing helpful comments. My heartfelt gratitude to Dr. Steve Striffler for thoroughly critiquing my work and serving as a mentor throughout my graduate studies.

Thank you, American Association for University Women, for awarding me a dissertation grant and rebuilding my confidence in writing, and the American Institute of Pakistan Studies, for providing me a research presentation grant. I am grateful to tutors at the University of Arkansas Writing Center, in particular, Dr. Robert Haslam, for their mentoring.

I am forever indebted to the free for all, public school and university systems of Pakistan that equipped me with the skills to excel in the United States. Thank you, Beenish Qazilbash, for your moral support and for always being a phone call away to get me in touch with people for interviews. Thank you, Kristi Arford, for your help in desperate times. I also thank Afaq Publishers in Karachi, Dawn newspapers, and Naveed Chacha for their support during fieldwork. Thank you, my wonderful teachers at St. Joseph's College for building my passion in the arts, and late Prof. Asrar Ahmed Siddiqui at the University of Karachi, who went out of his way to support my studies and career. Thank you, Cassia, for always being there for me, no matter what. Thank you, Ehsan Shakiba, for being a wonderful host. I also thank Joel for his intellectual, emotional, and aesthetic enrichment in my life. Heartiest thanks to my sister for her emotional and monetary support during my difficult graduate studies period. Last but not the least, I thank my parents, who smiled away all problems to open up the whole world to me.

CHAPTER 1

Introduction: Understanding Tradition, Modernity, and Class in Islamic Education

The expertise involved in making *chat*, a South Asian snack mix of dumplings, sauce, and crackers, lies in how perfectly one blends all the ingredients. In the summer of 2005, I visited a madrasa (religious seminary) to collect information for a pilot study on different school systems in Karachi. The school's administrator, Qari Mohammed Asghar, informed me that, in addition to working in the madrasa, he owned and ran a private school in another area. I asked him what courses were offered at that school. He said that his school offered a blend of all the government-approved secular subjects in a prestigious, private school environment, alongside Quranic memorization (*hifz*) and Quranic exegesis (*tafsir*) courses offered at the low-prestige madrasas. I asked him why he didn't open a madrasa instead of blending different curricula in a new type of private school. He replied, "Because people want chat!"[1]

The private schools Qari Mohammed Asghar referred to are what I term *Islamic schools*, an emergent, alternative form of religious schooling in Pakistan. In Urdu, people usually term these schools as *Islami* (Islamic) schools to distinguish them from madrasas. Though some Islamic schools existed in the 1990s, they have proliferated as an alternative educational regime since President Musharraf's crackdown on the madrasas in 2002. Post–9/11, Pakistani madrasas came under state scrutiny and were investigated by local and international media for promoting religious extremism. I went to Karachi in the summers of 2004 and 2005 to conduct pilot surveys on the madrasas and their clientele and to compare them to private secular schools and their clientele. I met parents who told me that they were choosing the private Islamic form of schooling because it provides traditional Islamic education as well as modern, secular education through the British O-level system. The O-level system, a colonial legacy, is more prestigious than the national system, known as the matriculation system. Curious about this unique religious educational phenomenon, I returned to Karachi in the summer of 2007 and lived there for a year exploring these *chat*-like schools that Qari Mohammad referred to and discovering why they are attractive for middle- and upper-class Karachi parents.

So far, no systematic study has been conducted on this education system in Pakistan. My aim here is to examine the emergence and continuous demand for this unique form of schooling among middle- and upper-class Karachiites from, first, a politico-historical perspective, and second, a socioeconomic perspective. For the first, I provide a background of the types of schools in the country to understand the gaps that these parochial schools are filling for urbanites. Next, I examine how state policies regarding the country's Islamic ideology and its role in education and lifestyle have influenced middle- and upper-class citizens' choice of Islamic schools. To this end, I trace the political story back to Zia-ul-Haq's martial law (1977–1988), which marked Cold War politics and the Afghan jihad against the Soviet Union in the 1970s. This era is important in understanding the politico-ideological environment in which many Pakistani parents choosing Islamic schools for their children today grew up. The era marked the first strong mullah-military alliance that weak democratic governments afterwards were not able to revert and that culminated in the proliferation of these schools under another martial law, that of Pervez Musharraf, from 1998 to 2008.

For the socioeconomic perspective, I examine private schools in relation to their facilities and English as the medium of instruction. Why are some parents no longer choosing private secular schools for their children? Why are they no longer creating Islamic subjectivities through madrasa education? Until a decade ago, Islamic education in the country was not associated with prestigious Western (O-level), secular education. How then are Islamic schools transforming the concept of Islamic education? These questions guide my narrative in the chapters that follow. In examining how private Islamic schooling caters to the religious, sectarian, class, ethnic, and political aspirations of Karachi parents, I attempt to widen the theoretical understanding of religion in the context of education and to add complexity to the analysis of Islamic education. I argue that different types of religious education create a variety of religious subjectivities. In addition, as the private Islamic schooling phenomenon highlights, religious education may create not only religious subjectivities but also subjectivities that are simultaneously class, ethnic, sectarian, gender, and political.

Spread over 2,193 square miles, Karachi's population is more than 18 million. As the largest city, seaport, and financial center of Pakistan, Karachi is home to diverse religions, Islamic sectarian traditions, ethnicities, and linguistic and communal groups. The diversity becomes increasingly complex with constant interprovincial migration for employment, refugee flows from Afghanistan, and the presence of international workers. I collected surveys and conducted formal and informal interviews with students, parents, teachers, and administrators in 15 Islamic schools. Out of these, two were run by the Ismaili Shiite community and three by the Twelver Shiite community. One was a non-Muslim Zoroastrian private religious school that I examined for comparison with Islamic schools. I discuss this school in chapter 4. The other nine Islamic schools that I visited belonged to Sunnis, who form the majority sect in Pakistan. Two were run by the Sunni linguistic business community, the Memons, and one by the followers of the Sunni subsect Ahl al-Hadith. Three belonged to the network of schools in Karachi established by the Sunni religious political party, Jamaat-e-Islami, whereas the rest were "commercial," meaning the administrations did not follow any sectarian or political ideology and operated more like private secular schools.

For comparative purposes, I collected data from five private secular schools and four male and female Sunni and Shiite madrasa branches. Because my aim was to examine the educational choices of middle- and upper-class urbanites and because madrasas are usually associated with the lower class, I concentrated on the Guidance Network of madrasas (pseudonym) in particular, for comparison with private Islamic and secular schools because it attracts educated middle- and upper-class children, housewives, and working women. By and large, I focused on female madrasas because, as a woman, male madrasas were not accessible, other than through the formal, supervised visits in which administrators met me indirectly through my male escort, my father.

The lower-middle-, upper-middle-, and upper-class families I spoke to, who can afford private school tuition, were largely salaried classes and small and big businesspersons. Similar to the private secular schooling system, private Islamic schooling also has its own hierarchy. Accordingly, some Islamic schools have been opened by entrepreneurs in upper-class areas and have better facilities. Others have been opened by entrepreneurs in middle- and lower-middle-class residential areas inside rented apartments. The ways in which class and religious subjectivities are negotiated in Islamic schools varies with the income group to which the schools cater.

To represent the various social backgrounds and class aspirations of the people who support Islamic schools and to understand how urban parents evaluate tuition costs and school facilities and how they associate prestige with Islamic schools in high-income areas, I visited schools in diverse income areas of Karachi—four low- to middle-income areas, five middle-income areas, three upper-middle income areas, and three high-income areas. My assessment of income areas in Karachi was solely based on housing and estate prices. Table 1.1 below lists the Islamic school with the corresponding income class of people who either lived in those areas or who were choosing an Islamic school there for social mobility, a topic that I discuss in more detail in chapter 5.

Besides diversity across income levels, Islamic schools are also diversified along political, ethnic, and sectarian lines. To obtain a nuanced picture of these schools, I collected data around three aspects of the schooling process. First, I examined the schools' daily routine, the basic pedagogical structure at the preprimary, primary (grades 1–5), and secondary (grades 6–10) levels. Second, my interest was to understand how aspirations and experiences of school administrators, staff, parents, and students define the *actual* pedagogical process to create various religious, sectarian, secular, gender, class, ethnic, and political subjectivities in the students. Third, I examined the school curricula to understand how it contributes to the creation of religious, modern, and gender subjectivities in the students. My interviews with administrators and teachers helped me understand their perceptions as conveyors of knowledge. With permission from the administrators, I talked with students during break times to understand how they perceive the school environment and missions—especially in comparison with private secular schools and madrasas—and how these perceptions align with the expectations of their families.

Table 1.1 Economic and Social Standing of Islamic Schools and Their Patrons Based on Income-Level Areas*

List of Areas	Monthly Income Range	Social Class
1. Federal B. Area 2. Guru Mandir 3. Lyari 4. Memon Colony	Rs.10–20,000, approximately US$100–200	Lower to middle
1. Gulshan-e-Iqbal 2. Gulistan-e-Jauhar 3. Nazimabad 4. North Nazimabad 5. Rizvia Society	Rs. 20–100,000, approximately US$2–1,000	Middle
1. P.E.C.H.S (Pakistan Employees Cooperative Housing Society) 2. Bahadurabad	Rs. 100,000–500,000, approximately US$1,000–5,000	Upper middle
1. Clifton 2. Defense 3. Malir Cantonment	Rs. 100,000 and above, in addition to inheritance. Approximately US$1,000 and above	Upper class

*This income range is a rough estimate based on a general social gentrification of areas by social class. As in many large cities, middle- and upper-class income areas show much fluctuation based on the age and education of the earners, inheritance, and foreign remittances.

At all three kinds of schools, most of my conversations with the informants were in Urdu, Pakistan's national language. However, English, Pakistan's official language, has a higher prestige value than Urdu, so, on several occasions, I used English to interview my informants at the English-medium Islamic schools and private secular schools and outside the school setting.

When I was not visiting schools, I spent time with families in which children went to Islamic schools. Through formal and informal interviews, I came to understand the aspirations, socioeconomic and educational backgrounds, and ideological and professional concerns of these families. In addition, I collected various textbooks, as well as pamphlets, advertisements, and brochures that could help me understand this schooling phenomenon.

Throughout the book, the schools' names have been replaced by categorical abbreviations to protect identities. For example, I use JIMA for Islamic schools established by alumni of madrasas operated by the Deobandi Sunni sect, which follows the religious political party of Pakistan, the Jamaat-e-Islami.

Anthropologists born in the East and trained in the West who have observed their native societies have shared the experience of how "being home" played out during fieldwork. Srinivas states that mere nativeness does not provide the anthropologist immunity to the complexities of his or her own culture.[2] Describing his experience of researching in Mysore as a native Brahmin Hindu, the author reveals how some Brahmins objected that he was not following rituals particular to his caste in the conventional ways and was socializing with the lower castes. In my case, being raised in Karachi as a product of one of its private secular schools, the social and educational atmospheres of my field site were familiar to me. Yet the minute I told interviewees that I was examining schools as part of a doctoral research project in the United States, they would ask, "So are you with the FBI or the CIA?" It was hard to convince people that the United States had not sent me back to obtain inside information on the activities of religious schools in Pakistan. It was only when I began to highlight details about the middle-class neighborhood in which I was living with my parents that middle-class families began trusting me with information. Once, I was taking speedy notes about *nazira* (Quranic recitation) at an Islamic school when the proprietor, who was highly suspicious of my motives for coming back from the United States, sent his wife over to me. She sat next to me and read my notes out of the corner of her eye. I asked her whether she would like to give me her opinion and asked her name. She said it was Nadra, which means priceless. I wrote *nazira*. She corrected me, and I apologized, explaining that it had only been two weeks since I had returned and that I could really use her help in coming back to my language and culture. "Yes, you must have lost plenty of it. Come to our school often and you'll relearn it."[3] Such moments came as a relief to me, because in those moments my informants were able to see me as someone whom they could save from Western culture and re-enculturate in Pakistani culture, rather than someone who was there to find out their secrets and relate them to the American government.

My morality in the United States was checked with questions such as, "There are Muslim students' associations there. Are you a member or not?" "Did you live in the dorm there?" When I would satisfy my interviewees that I lived far away from the dorm culture that many

Pakistani families with relatives studying in the United States conceive as the epitome of demoralization in the West, I would next be asked if my roommates were Muslim. These were some of the ways in which people regularly ascertained my religiosity and my closeness to Pakistan's cultural values before trusting me with any information.

Similar to what Arab women anthropologists have noted about their fieldwork experiences at home, in Pakistan, I became much more aware of my femininity.[4] The expectations of informants, neighbors, family, and friends to behave like a proper Pakistani woman were stifling at first. As a young, single woman out asking questions, I was under constant pressure to represent the moral upbringing of my family, in particular, my father. Very often I would ask about the school and instead hear, "And your father lets you do this?" I transformed my gestures, postures, and style of walking to suit the tastes of what men and women wanted to see: sometimes a daughter; sometimes a young woman who is not only less knowledgeable than the men, but also the least knowledgeable among women because she is still single; and sometimes a woman who desired to study Islamic education to become more pious, like the women she sought to interview. I learned that my informants felt more prepared to meet someone with my background than I felt in meeting them. Sometimes, it was hard to convince people that I was collecting information only for my studies and not for intelligence services. At other times, it was hard to convince people that I was a serious fieldworker, not some native girl who was fooling people by asking them personal, financial, and professional questions. I learned to cover my head all the time and, for one year, bought and wore only the clothes that were full-sleeved, not bright in color, and did not follow the latest fashion. In sum, a native anthropologist often has greater disadvantage because he or she has stayed far away from the parts of culture to which he or she does not relate. Having to immerse in these areas of culture as an observer then becomes a struggle to unlearn one's cultural ways in order to relearn them from the point of view of the culture objectified.

Without a husband or a child, my only way of gaining status, prestige, respect, and legitimacy was by relying on my education. Very often it ushered an insistence on the part of the informants to answer my questions in English, using a Pakistani prestige criterion to impress me. It would take some counter insistence on my part to demonstrate that I could still speak in Urdu to build rapport. Contrastingly, on other occasions, my native Urdu accent made people think that I was lying about studying in the United States. To earn serious recognition in such cases, I randomly began decorating my Urdu with English, a *burgher* trait that always discomforted me, and hoped that the accent came out as American as possible. The language switching worked like magic, and I was allowed to begin structured interviews in Urdu. Interestingly, upper-class families remained unapproachable until my American-accented English helped me find a job as an English-language instructor in Clifton, an upper-middle- to upper-class area of Karachi. As people came to know that I was working on a doctoral degree in the United States, the fact that I resided in a middle-class area became less important, and upper-class families began allowing me to approach them with questions as an equal. Thus, it was only by using native subjectivities as trump cards on certain occasions and foreign subjectivities on other occasions that I was able to navigate as a *native* anthropologist.

Doing fieldwork in Karachi, I relearned much of the protocol of engaging in formal conversation in Pakistan while displaying proper Islamic body language, gestures, and greetings. As my familiarity with the schools and my informants increased, my Urdu became increasingly formal, and I learned how to frequently infuse my speech with *Inshallah* ("if God wills," used to suggest that the future is uncertain) and *Mashallah* ("as God has willed," an Islamic phrase used to admire things). Because the Arabic language signifies pure Islamic language and Persian less so because of its association with Shiism, a minority sect in Pakistan, I also had to learn to replace many Persian origin words in Urdu with the Arabic origin/Islamic ones, especially in greetings like *Khuda hafiz* (*Khuda* signifying God in Persian), a farewell greeting replaced by the Arabic version, *Allah hafiz*.

My sectarian identity became important and politicized inside both Islamic schools and madrasas. I began by offering silence when people asked if I was Shiite or Sunni, because it did not matter that I was not prejudiced against the country's Shiite minority. After all, I was navigating in Karachi, where violence against minority sects and religious communities keeps them alert at all times. I would be a Shiite at a Shiite Islamic school and a Sunni at the Sunni ones. I would say I believed in "just Islam" to appease the puritanical Deobandis among whom many think that the other Sunni sect, Barelvis, celebrate post-Islamic practices. I must admit always living in the guilt and fear that some counter-checking would reveal that I had told the Barelvis about my sympathies for Barelvi Islam.

One day, when I was talking around my subsectarian identity, a Shiite Islamic school principal, Fatima, looked into my eyes, lifted her hand, and asked, "Just tell me if you are a Sayyid by any chance" [The Sayyid are people accepted as Prophet Muhammad's descendants through his grandsons, Hasan and Husayn, who were the sons of his daughter Fatima Zahra and son-in-law Ali ibn Abi Talib].[5] I never knew I would use my most insignificant marker, that I was apparently half Sayyid, until that day. On my next visit, sipping Mirinda in Fatima's office while waiting for literature to be brought out by her assistant, when I informed her that some relatives on my mother's side did claim to be Sayyid, she said, "Good enough. It doesn't make you a weaker Sayyid. You're still amongst the blessed, chosen family of Allah."[6] In the minds of many Pakistani Shiites, Sayyid equals Shiite. When I visited the school again the next day, no suspicious eyes watched me as I peeked into the corridors and opened up textbooks. I sensed that Fatima had passed on the news to her colleagues quickly. There were many other moments in which I wished to live the other illusion: that of a non-native researcher, a foreign face who would receive straightforward answers to her questions without her native ideologies and stances put under scrutiny.

Being a native and an observer did not simply require immersion and adjustments when dealing with the people associated with Islamic schools and madrasas. I met many Karachi leftists in family, friends, and some elite informants' circles who thought that I had returned as the stereotype of a Pakistani American who, in diaspora, had begun revisiting her roots, wanting to learn more about her native culture. After spending mornings at madrasas, where I constantly debated whether my mannerisms had convinced people that I was religious enough, I had to spend many evenings with friends and sympathizers who, learning of my fieldwork, would conduct psychotherapic conversations with me, pointing me toward the Arts Council in Karachi, latest theater performances, and poetry recitations, and I would often be asked, "So, do you still want to return to those people [conservatives]?"[7] As I reconciled the worlds of people associated with religious schooling with that of those reminding me that it was all a farce, I was frequently flustered, but only more awakened to the diversity that signifies mainstream urban communities in Pakistan and the absurdness of the monolithic notion of "native anthropologist."

Writing about the scandalization of Pakistani madrasas in connection with the September 11, 2001, attacks in the United States, Christopher Candland wrote, "It is a mistake to assume that only Islamic boarding schools are involved in Islamic education. Thousands of private schools . . . impart a predominantly Islamic education. Yet very little attention has been focused on the curriculum or pedagogy in these sectarian and political party oriented private schools."[8] No body of literature, apart from Internet blogs and opinion pieces in English and Urdu newspapers, exists on these schools, and the government lists of private schools simply lump the Islamic schools together with private secular schools. This book is the first endeavor to understand the reasons why some Pakistani urban families are patronizing this new kind of privileged, private and traditional, religious education system and, by doing so, contributing to new ways of understanding the place of religion in the Pakistani urban landscape. Since Islamic schools are an emergent phenomenon, it is important to point out that this study provides an incomplete picture primarily for two reasons. First, many Islamic schools opened inside bungalows and apartments in the middle- and lower-middle-class neighborhoods and closed down between 2004 and 2008, thus changing the impact of these schools on Karachi's landscape. This is not unknown in small, private, secular school enterprises. Second, I did my fieldwork during a time of political turmoil and revolutionary change in the country. When I began in 2007, the Musharraf government was still busy cracking down on religious extremism amid "Go Musharraf Go!" demonstrations all over the country—the most powerful of those being the demonstrations staged by the lawyers and judges sacked by Musharraf. In January 2008, elections resulted in the restoration of democracy, and the new government's immediate attention was set on combating the infiltration of the Taliban in northwestern Pakistan. My fieldwork ended at the time the new government had just allocated 7 percent of the national budget to education, the largest in the country's history. Nevertheless, the educational sector most affected by the educational policies of the previous and the current government remains that of public schools, and not the private ones that are the preferred schools for middle and upper-class urbanites and upper-class urbanites.

Overview of the Chapters

The private Islamic educational experiment is not unique to Pakistan, but is rather a growing trend in other Muslim countries as well. A few systematic studies have been conducted in Indonesia, Malaysia, Thailand, Egypt, and India on the emergence and patronization of such hybrid schools.[9] In chapter 2, "Situating the Private Islamic Schooling Trend in Pakistan," I analyze private Islamic schooling in Pakistan from a global perspective by comparing the pedagogical ideologies and politico-historical factors that have led to the emergence and popularity of such schools in Pakistan to their counterparts in Indonesia, Malaysia, Thailand, Egypt, and India.

Examining the multiple subjectivities that private Islamic schools construct in their students meant that I examined, on the one hand, literature in educational anthropology that would help me analyze the dynamics of the pedagogical process and the class subjectivities that schools create and, on the other hand, literature in the anthropology of Islam that would help me analyze concepts such as Islamic tradition, secularism, and modernity in the context of education. In the second part of chapter 2, I bring into conversation theoretical debates and case studies in the anthropology of education and Islam to stress how their blending can project a more nuanced understanding of Islamic social practice in the educational domain.

Islamic schooling is unique as it is the first experiment in blending traditional madrasa style education with modern, secular education in the private educational system. Why was a need felt to do such an experiment? In chapter 3, "The Educational System of Pakistan and the Place of Private Islamic Schooling," I address this question by first providing some background on the state of public and private secular schools and madrasas in Pakistan to contextualize the current Islamic schooling trend. I then examine the social and professional significance of English versus Urdu medium instruction in schools and that of the prestigious and foreign O-level versus the less prestigious and local Matric system of examination and how these factors and the government's changing policy on the role of Islam in the social and educational lives of Pakistanis have shaped the schooling choices of urban middle- and upper-class families. Finally, with the help of interviews, I highlight the class, religious, cultural, and other socioeconomic concerns that are attracting Karachi parents to the new Islamic schools and how its founders are describing the schools' missions.

The basic educational structure at Islamic schools may be similar. However, the pedagogical missions and activities in each Islamic school is different, based on the producers of knowledge in these schools who guide its ideology. In chapter 4, "Examining Diversity in Private Islamic Schools," I discuss the diversity among Islamic schools' missions and pedagogies.

What is the daily routine at an Islamic school like? What are the pedagogical features in these schools? In what ways do the school pedagogies construct Islamic, gender, and class ideologies? How do people associated with the schools—school administrators, teachers, students, and parents—describe the educational process? What kinds of religious, class, gender, and national subjectivities do they seek to create, and how do people's narratives and classroom dynamics and the schools' missions varyingly construct these subjectivities? In chapter 5, "Knowledge at Play," I address these questions by presenting ethnographic and interview data from four schools, two opened by madrasa alumni (one Sunni, one Shiite) and two by entrepreneurs not trained in theology (one catering to upper- and one to middle-class Karachiites). I chose the schools because they represented the widest diversity of Islamic schools. Finally, I examine how the schools' textbooks contribute to the schools' mission of constructing particular Islamic and gender subjectivities in the students.

In sum, what follows is the first attempt to bring to light a new educational trend in religious schooling in Pakistan. As much as the September 11, 2001, attacks on the United States by religious extremists have ensued investigations on religious education in Pakistan, the phenomenon that has been overlooked is how urban, educated, middle- and upper-class Pakistanis choose nonmilitant and moderate forms of religious education over education in some radical madrasas. The purpose of my fieldwork narrative is to underscore that Pakistanis promoting religious education not only seek to create religious subjectivities in their children, but also those that are socially prestigious and professionally promising. I argue that middle- and upper-class parents' choice of the new Islamic schools is made with an acute understanding of the religious image of Pakistanis in the post-9/11 international community and the state's changing educational and religious policies.

CHAPTER 2

Situating the Islamic Schooling Trend in Pakistan

In the summers of 2004 and 2005, I visited Pakistan to conduct a pilot study on religious education in Pakistan. Despite being a native anthropologist, I was not better informed than the international media and only examined religious education and practice inside madrasas. As I collected comparative information from private secular schools to understand differences in their pedagogical methods from those of the madrasas, I noticed the growth of a private Islamic kind of schooling. I was curious to know whether this educational phenomenon, that I later returned to Pakistan to study in detail, was present elsewhere in the world. I found that, although no systematic research has yet been done on Islamic schools in Pakistan, they are a fast-growing trend among majority and minority Muslim communities in various Asian and Middle Eastern countries. Although a few studies exist, there is a dearth of systematic examination of these modern Islamic schools. Parochial schools have also become widespread among diasporic Muslim communities in the United States and Europe. My second task was to find a theoretical grounding for terms such as *Islamic way of life, traditional Islamic education, modern secular schooling,* and *moderate Islam* that administrators, teachers, and parents used frequently during my conversations with them in Karachi. This chapter undertakes the following discussions:

1. The private Islamic educational experiment is not unique to Pakistan, but is rather a growing trend in Indonesia, Thailand, Egypt, and India. In this chapter, I compare the Islamic school in Pakistan that emerged as an effort to sustain traditional Islamic

education and blend it with modern needs to similar, ongoing reform initiatives in these four countries. This is by no means a comprehensive global survey on this educational trend, nor a comprehensive account of the histories, politics, and socioeconomic conditions that have informed these reform initiatives. Rather, it is to take attention away from madrasas and either orthodox interpreters of Islamic tradition or extremists as the only focus of study to one that understands challenging, alternate discourses on religious practice and education of mainstream Muslims.
2. Next, I discuss the theoretical sources that helped me analyze the private Islamic schooling phenomenon in Pakistan. I attempt to borrow from sources in both Islamic anthropology and educational anthropology to construct a theoretical framework for analyzing how the concepts of Islamic tradition, secular and modern education, and class are fused in private Islamic schooling in an attempt to create multiple subjectivities in the students. In doing so, I point out the gaps in the existing body of literature in these areas, which I attempt to fill through my own examination of the private Islamic schooling phenomenon in Karachi.

1. Pakistani Islamic Schools in Relation to Their Global Prototypes

The Islamic schools in urban Pakistan represent an emergent schooling trend that is reflective of similar educational experiments by Muslim communities in other parts of Asia and the Middle East.

1a) Private Islamic Schooling Trend in Indonesia

In Indonesia, the *pesantrens* or Islamic boarding schools have grown for many of the same reasons that they have grown in Pakistan. *Pesantrens* are similar to the Pakistani madrasas in that they provide free education from morning to evening, with free room and board. However, whereas students in most of the Pakistani madrasas have been dependent on private donations from countries such as the United States, Saudi Arabia, and Iran until the present, *pesantren* students work in the rice fields and other plantations to support their education.[1]

The *pesantren* schools were the only form of education in Indonesia until the modern system of schooling was introduced by the

Dutch. In the second half of the twentieth century, the question arose as to whether *pesantrens* are compatible with the modern Dutch schools and prepare students to compete in the job market. This led many *pesantrens* to incorporate secular subjects alongside Islamic subjects. The addition of state-recognized curricula has led to greater government control of the schools.[2] It has also made the *pesantrens* operate more like the Pakistani Islamic schools because now parents generally pay room and board and tuition. The time that the students used to spend working is now spent in secular education. Traditional *pesantrens* now operate both as government-sponsored Islamic middle schools and private Islamic boarding schools in urban and rural areas.

Although in certain structural and pedagogical ways, the *pesantrens* are similar to the Islamic schools I examined in Karachi, they are different in two ways. First, *pesantrens* are not the new, reformed forms of madrasas. Instead, after Musharraf's crackdown on madrasas, the Islamic schools were initiated by businessmen and madrasa alumni and popularized by middle- and upper-class urbanites because they offered a moderate alternative to the extremist madrasas brought under governmental, public, media, and international scrutiny, as discussed in chapter 1. Second, unlike the *pesantrens*, the Pakistani Islamic schools are not government-sponsored. Similar to the *pesantrens* and the private secular schools in Pakistan, Islamic schools teach the secular curricula prescribed by the government, but their kind of Islamic tradition is more diverse and class-based, as I highlight in chapters 4 and 5.

1b) Private Islamic Schooling Trend in Thailand

In southern Thailand, there are three kinds of schools. Similar to the public schools in Pakistan, the government schools in Thailand teach the national curriculum, along with Islamic education, or Islamiat as it is called in Pakistani public and private secular schools. The medium of instruction is Thai, similar to the national language, Urdu, in Pakistani government schools. In addition, there are the *pondok* schools, which are equivalent to Pakistani madrasas in that they are room-and-board dormitories in which boys learn from a the local *imam* (religious teacher). In Pakistani madrasas, learning the ancient Arabic and to some extent Persian treatises of the fourteenth century

Dars-e-Nizami curriculum is an essential part of learning. In southern Thailand *pondoks*, learning Jawi, an Arabic script that was once used to write Malay, is important. Unlike the recent emergence of private Islamic schools in Pakistan, which proliferated mainly in reaction to the insistence of the Musharraf government to incorporate science and math in madrasa curriculum, private Islamic schools in southern Thailand proliferated in the 1960s, when *pondoks* were asked to reform their curriculum. These private Islamic schools were taken as models to improve pedagogy, to put an end to rote memorization of religious subjects, and to incorporate math, science, civic education, computer science, and other subjects in the curriculum.

Sometimes, private Islamic schools in Bangkok also operate as evening and weekend schools for students who attend government schools. Nevertheless, as I will discuss in relation to curriculum in Islamic schools in Pakistan, the educational blend in private Islamic schools is aimed not only at blending religious and secular education but also at adding a religious dimension to all subjects. Arabic is one of the mediums of instruction. Unlike a regional or ethnic language, Malay, the official and national language Thai is promoted alongside Arabic. Similarly, a modern curriculum other than the fourteenth-century Dars-e-Nizami syllabus taught in madrasas, is promoted in private Islamic schools in Pakistan. In addition, Islamiat is often taught in the language of prestige, English, which is also the country's official language. In this way, the curriculum in Bangkok and Karachi private Islamic schools is standardized to meet state requirements and professional needs.

In southern Thailand, some reformism and blending of secular and religious education has also been aimed at higher education by Ismail Lutfi, who received his doctorate in sharia (moral code and religious law of Islam) in 1986. His institute is known as Yala Islamic University. He is popular for openly embracing technology while teaching traditional madrasa subjects in Islam. While this has caused much mistrust and suspicion among traditional clerics, it has also not given him much favor in the Western media, which has regarded his reform efforts as a cover to promote a Wahhabi agenda. Nevertheless, his reformed Islamic curriculum includes academic subjects, such as business, technology, finance, and the social sciences. However, efforts in Thailand are not similar to the private Islamic schools in Pakistan, where the effort is to synthesize public and private schools secular curriculum in grades 1–10 with madrasa curriculum, so as to modernize the latter in a moderate fashion and close the gap between secular schools and madrasa graduates in the job market.

In chapter 4, I focus on the diversity in private Islamic schools of Pakistan based on the educational backgrounds, commercial interests, sectarian, and political interests of the entrepreneurs and patron families. The Thai private Islamic schools are no different. In Chiang Mai, which represents half of the country's Muslim population and is largely Chinese, followed by South Asian, private Islamic schools are few. The schools largely represent Chiang Mai's diverse Muslim demographic, which has made the minority communities more concerned about continuing Islamic traditions in the country than defining them along sectarian lines.[3] Santi Suksha School in Ciang Mai, for example, offers both religious and secular education, but it operates more like a private secular school, in which people of all faiths can receive instruction in their own faith.

Whether the Malay Muslim community of southern Thailand patronizes private Islamic schools more than the Chiang Mai Muslim community or not, the Thai counterpart of Islamic schools I saw in Pakistan provide an alternative to traditional madrasas as a way to reform Islamic education. Furthermore, the diversity of these schools in Thailand and Pakistan point to the diverse subjectivities created through Islamic schooling that are a result of the negotiation of pedagogies, curriculum choices, and patron communities. Reform experiments in the two countries may have originated under different political, historical, and social contexts. However, together they represent efforts on the part of citizens to represent themselves as part of a global professional community by disassociating their traditional Islamic education from extremism and the state's changing educational and religious policies. As Hefner notes, "Islamic education is characterized not by lock-step uniformity but by a teeming plurality of actors, institutions, and ideas."[4]

1c) Private Islamic Schooling Trend in Egypt

A trend toward private Islamic education, similar to what I examined in Pakistan, has developed in Egypt in the last two decades and has been studied by anthropologists.[5] Herrera's study of Egyptian Islamic education provides useful insight into the Islamic schooling phenomenon in Pakistan, because she not only provides the detailed political and historical backgrounds in which these schools have emerged but also presents ethnographic information and data from interviews with people inside the schools. She divides the Egyptian Islamic schools according to their pedagogical trend into three types: (A) private Islamic English-language schools, (B) extremist private Islamic schools, and (C) private schools of Islamic nongovernmental organizations (NGOs).

Herrera's case study of type-A schools describes the school "as an Islamic alternative to the prestigious Christian schools which many of the Muslim and Christian elite attended largely because of their emphasis on foreign languages."[6] The owner of the school aimed to equip students with proficient English skills and a first-rate education. Students were prepared to enter the foreign business community, working and living abroad, and conveying the principles of Islam in the West, in an effort to gain acceptance of Islam. The type-B schools are called extremist by local Egyptians because they are "owned and operated by individuals who are involved in Islamic-opposition politics and are used as a means of cultivating and channeling forms and expressions of political dissent."[7] These schools are inspired by the political and ideological convictions of the Muslim Brotherhood in Egypt. The schools are a site for dawa (Islamic propagation), which will enable the Muslim society to come out of dormancy as a result of the state's manipulation, a dormancy equated to *jahiliyya* or the pre-Islamic state of ignorance, and return to true faith. The type-C Islamic schools combine religious and secular education and teach it with a heavy emphasis on the Arabic language to students who come to the private NGOs' educational facilities. The school's mission is to teach students how to internalize Islam rather than just study it like a curriculum subject, which is how it is taught in the government schools. The schools pay no attention to the English language or computer training. However, parents continue to send their children to Islamic NGO–run private schools because they are more affordable than other private schools.[8]

Herrera's study is the only anthropological study available on private Islamic schooling at this time. However, the schools she examined in Cairo differ from those in Karachi on several grounds. First, the variety in Karachi Islamic schools is based on differences in class and prestige, sectarian ideologies, ethnic interests, and political affiliations of the entrepreneurs and patrons. Although in Karachi these schools can be broadly divided into puritanical and liberal schools, the puritanical ones are not part of any extremist religio-political movements, as is the case in Egypt. They do not oppose the state but rather stand as an alternative mode of Islamic schooling that does not evoke the religious extremism associated with Pakistani madrasas post–9/11 attacks on the United States, nor censors Islamic education at the expense of a Western model of secular education, as is the case in the private secular schools that follow the British O-level syllabus and examination system for ninth and tenth graders. Also, in Pakistan, no NGOs have yet developed a formal system of private Islamic schooling. I visited an Islamic school located in the middle-class neighborhood of Gulshan-e-Iqbal, Karachi, run by a couple who are graduates of secular colleges and universities. I asked Nadra, the wife and vice principal of the school, where the funds to establish the school came from. She replied that the school had been started through a charity with personal funds and shares from the endowments and private funds received by the madrasas with which the school was affiliated. I asked Nadra if that made her Islamic school an NGO. She said, "No! Not at all! NGOs promote secular values. This school is run through Islamic charity that every Muslim gives in the form of zakat" [percentage of charity binding on every Muslim and received annually by the state].[9] Nadra thinks of NGOs as the secular modernists, whom she cannot conceive as promoting religion. While doing a comparative examination of the madrasas, I heard similar criticism from the teachers about NGO educational programs. Even though religious political parties such as the Jamaat-e-Islami in Pakistan operate their own NGOs where they train the homeless in Quranic reading, NGOs in Pakistan run private schools only on the pedagogical pattern of secular public and private schools.

Third, English-medium education that is unique to Herrera's type-A school is not unique to Pakistani Islamic schools, because English is also the medium of instruction in private secular schools. English proficiency is an important status symbol and required for many domestic and international jobs and is promoted by the Pakistani Islamic schools, while Arabic is significant as the language of Islam. In this way, Islamic schools promote an Islamic education that simultaneously creates class, modern, and religious subjectivities. Moreover, Islamic schools, just like the private secular schools, are always in competition with each other based on how many extra computer lab, sports, and other facilities they can offer. The Karachi Islamic schools I examined are also different from the type-A Egyptian schools because they are an indigenous concept, and their mission is to enable students to fill the ideological and social needs of their urban lives, rather than prepare them for the diaspora. According to Nadra, "We are trying to offer O-level education, but the environment in our school is *decent*. It is not like the Western style environment that you find in some private secular schools."[10] Nadra's speech shows how English-medium private secular schools try to compete, but, according to her, Islamic schools come off better than the private secular schools because they impart Western education while reinforcing Islam daily. In addition, all Islamic schools in Pakistan, whether opened by madrasa alumni or other entrepreneurs, are commercial enterprises. However, the degree to which they are commercial depends on their fee structure, the area in which they are located, and whether they are affiliated with a madrasa that provides some funding.

1d) Private Islamic Schooling Trend in India

Similar to their Pakistani counterparts, madrasas in India teach a variation of the Dars-e-Nizami syllabus and are largely attended by the poor, who are looking for room and board, which has deviated middle- and upper-class Muslims overwhelmingly to private secular schools. This is not unlike Pakistan, where the use of madrasas as breeding grounds to produce jihadis for the American-Russian Cold War in Afghanistan during the Zia-ul-Haq era led middle- and upper-class citizens to patronize private secular schools. The increased Hinduization of public and private education because of the state's soft spot for the Hindutva-brand nationalism, an ideology with a mission to create a Hindu nation that is run by the umbrella organization of this ideology, the Sangh Parivar, is alienating its Muslim communities. Furthermore, local Muslim reformers call this trend zeheni irtidad, or intellectual apostasy, which happens when Muslims detach themselves from their faith and community.[11] Unlike Pakistan, madrasas do not receive state endowment in India, which makes modernization incentives trickier for the minorities. In response to this scenario, reform efforts in India have led to the patronization of schools that blend secular academic subjects with madrasa curriculum. The schools are becoming a means to save the country's Muslim minority from further marginalization in the educational and professional sphere.

In this backdrop, and gradually since the demolition of Babri Masjid in 1992 by right-wing Hindu political party affiliates in India, modern private Islamic schools have started emerging that offer both secular and religious curriculum. The most notable among them are schools established by the Jamaat-e-Islami social and religious organization, which is also an active political party in Pakistan. Many of the private Islamic schools I examined in Pakistan have been opened by Jamaat-e-Islami and are very often run by alumni of their brand of madrasas. These tend to range in their adherence to an Islamic code of appearance and behavior from a stricter, madrasa-like environment while following the national curriculum to others that operate more like private secular schools. I met the late Mr. Khusro, a Jamaat-e-Islami activist who ran a private Islamic school close to his residence and asked him why he moved toward these schools in his eighties. He responded:

> Our guide, Maududi [Muslim revivalist in British India and later in Pakistan who founded and led the Jamaat-e-Islami], had already laid the framework for it in the forties. This idea predates Pakistan [1947]. Being the visionary he was, he said that if we want to lead the world we should teach both Islamic and other subjects in schools from primary to secondary levels [grades 1–10]. The Islamic environment would ensure that professionally competent citizenry that could bring about a competent government for the Islamic state would be created. We are the ones now understanding what he envisioned. He prophesied that if we didn't create these types of schools, it would lead to our complete downfall. We didn't listen to him then and now see what we have put ourselves in. The madrasas are fighting with the government. The government as usual is not sincere, but it has made a mockery of our cherished, legacy madrasa tradition. So, now we are making a small effort here with this school to realize his vision.[12]

It must be noted here that, envisioning the Islamic blend of modern schooling, Maududi himself was not educated in a madrasa. This is true for the majority of entrepreneurs of the modern Islamic schools in Pakistan, in which finances are not tied to the madrasa budget. Mr. Khusro's account points to reform and modernization happening on a much smaller scale among Jamaat-e-Islami–affiliated Muslim communities in some parts of India. The Darsgah, established in 1949 as a model for private Islamic schools, after closing in the 1960s, has now been revamped to provide both religious and public school education for grades 1–5, a model that has inspired more than 1,600 similar schools in India. The Jamiatul Falah is another initiative with modern schooling coupled with madrasa-style theology training spanning fourteen years and including the alim (Islamic scholar) and *fazil* courses offered at Indian and Pakistani madrasas and equivalent to tenth-grade and twelfth-grade certificates of secular schools, respectively. The Indian and Pakistani models of Jamaat-e-Islami private Islamic schools commonly reduce the Islamic curriculum to "just Islam," that is Quran and *hadith* (sayings and conduct of Prophet Muhammed); they welcome people of all *maslak* (school of thought in Islamic law), though students enrolled in the Pakistani model are predominantly Sunni. Similar to Pakistani private Islamic schools, these efforts in broadening madrasa-education curriculum through blended schooling allows graduates to join public and private universities and professions outside religion. However, because experiments similar to Jamiatul Falah are still being conducted within the parameters of madrasa education, the extent to which the quality of their national curriculum is on par with other schools in India varies. Still, while private Islamic schools have opened up in the country, many madrasas have also incorporated English-medium secular education, such as the Markaz ul-Maarif Education and Research Center, Mumbai, or the Ummahat al-Mu'minin Girls' Higher Secondary School, where Islamic education is blended with regular schooling.

Schools closer to the Pakistani parochial schooling model have also opened in Kerala, Hyderabad, Aurangabad, Jalgaon, and New Delhi by Jamaat-e-Islami and other organizations in India. Similar to their Pakistani counterparts, which mark themselves as different from madrasas by using English, the socially prestigious language, as the medium of instruction, some of these schools in India are English-medium. Experiments such as the International Islamic School established by Zakir Naik—an Islamic scholar popular in India, Pakistan, Bangladesh, and South Asian communities—operate more like private secular schools: English-medium, charging a substantial fee, following standard national curriculum standards, and properly furnished and air-conditioned to attract middle and upper classes.[13]

Experimental Islamic schools are growing in India, a country in which Muslims constitute the largest religious minority. The Mappila Muslims of Malabar, Sunni by sect, make up almost a quarter of Kerala's population. The religious education system of these Muslims, from the 1950s onward, was at stake due to calls for modernization. This turned the attention of the Samastha Kerala Jamiyyathul Ulama (SKJU), an organization of traditional Sunni religious clerics, which then facilitated the integration of religious and secular education at the primary level. However, the organization continued the secular-religious dichotomy at higher levels until the 1970s. Parents who wanted to make their children religious scholars sent them to Islamic colleges, where learning was limited to traditional religious subjects. The result was incompetent religious graduates who were unable to carry forward their religious ethos. Similarly, in Pakistan, madrasas were revitalized under Zia-ul-Haq in the 1980s to produce soldiers for the war in Afghanistan against the Soviets, which turned the students into militants who were incompetent in the job market. This incompetency turned thousands of madrasa graduates into religious extremists, thus scandalizing the image of religious education in the country.[14]

In the 1970s, scholars of the Samastha responded to this issue by trying to synthesize both streams of knowledge. A private Islamic school called Dar ul-Huda was established in 1986 to achieve this goal. Today, Darul-Huda offers a twelve-year course, in which the curriculum integrates religious subjects, comparative studies of various religions, and secular subjects. According to a graduate, Hudawi, interviewed by the Indian sociologist Yoginder Sikand, Darul-Huda catered to bright students and selected them based on merit at a time when religious education in South India was the choice of poor students.[15] Admissions based on merit encouraged many rich and highly educated families to enroll their children in these schools. The Darul-Huda has now expanded into a university chain with approximately twenty colleges that follow the same syllabus under a coordination committee.

The Pakistani Islamic schools are operating in a Muslim majority society, and Darul-Huda's struggle is to build a positive image of a minority community. Compared to the madrasas, the Pakistani private Islamic education is a middle- and upper-class phenomenon that is prestigious because of the O-level education and is highly sought by parents from these classes.

Chapter 4 addresses the diversity of private Islamic schools in Pakistan to highlight that the choice is not always based on religious concerns of middle- and upper-class parents. For some parents, Islamic schools within a certain vicinity means that their children can seek upward social mobilization by enrolling in them. For others, an Islamic school is better because it is cheaper than a private secular school in the area. This points to the diversity in subjectivities created through these schools, depending on the ways in which its Islamic atmosphere is defined and communicated in pedagogy and through the aspirations of its patrons. Rucha Ambikar points to a similar phenomenon in relation to private right-wing Hindu schools, of which there are currently over 18,000 throughout India seeking to construct a youth committed to Hindutva. Ambikar argues that Muslim students are ready to ignore the extreme Hindu ideals propagated in these schools and moral education that requires the memorization of prayers in Sanskrit and school assembly prayers to the Hindu goddess of learning, Sarasvati, because they are private, yet much cheaper than private secular schools, and offer state-approved standard curriculum, including computer education and English, which are class-elevating and professionally promising. In chapter 5, I highlight how private Islamic schools in Pakistan's urban centers give modern education an Islamic flavor by incorporating Quranic recitations and by infusing secular subject content with an Islamic message. However, Ambikar's study on religious education in India highlights an important feature of Islamic schooling in Karachi: factors such as class elevation and economic concerns must be examined to no lesser degree in people's motivation to seek Islamic schooling for their children than they are in examination of any other type of schooling.[16] Under Zia-ul-Haq, the country's educational and social system was Islamized, so much so that history, social studies, and Pakistan studies curriculum from grades one through ten, and even at the university level, was reduced to teaching only the Islamic past of the country when it was a part of India and all the way back to the Islamic caliphates formed after Prophet Muhammad's death. All references to its Hindu, Buddhist, and Christian heritage were erased. However, contrary to the Hindutva school curriculum, in which only Hindu rule is taught in history lessons and missions including securing Hindu lands in Pakistan are taught, Islamic schools in Pakistan, which are not controlled by the country's extremist right-wingers, are reversing the curricula to include mention of the country's multi-religious and cultural heritage and demographic, an emphasis I return to in chapter 5.

In the case of *pesantrens,* Egyptian Islamic schools, and Darul-Huda, the traditional religious education in the colonial era was a mode of preserving a local, Muslim identity. In the eighteenth-century British colonial India, madrasas served to preserve Muslim identity. During the cold war, the madrasas in Pakistan became breeding grounds for training fighters for the Afghan war against the Soviet occupation. As a result, madrasa teaching became radicalized, and in 2002, the Musharraf government cracked down on them to modernize their curricula. The Islamic schools emerged in this scenario.

Between August and December 2007, I asked fifteen administrators, teachers, eighth- to tenth-grade students (fourteen to sixteen years of age) and their parents in Islamic schools if they supported the Musharraf government's policy to crack down on the madrasas. Eight supported the policy to reform but replied that the traditional institutions of Islamic learning should never be closed down. Out of these, five added that reforming madrasas is good but to do it in support of America is treachery to Pakistan and Islam. Four out of fifteen wanted Musharraf to end his martial law and come into politics as a legitimate civilian before shutting down Islam's ancient centers of learning that had produced innumerable political scientists, scholars, thinkers, poets, and national heroes. Seven added that the extremist madrasas were military institutions to begin with. Similar to the role of madrasas during the British colonization of India, the Islamic schools are a mode of preserving national, political, and religious identities for Pakistan's urban citizens in a post–September 11 socio-political environment in which Pakistani madrasas have been defamed in Western media and by the Musharraf government's crackdown on the madrasas. The spread of the private, hybrid Islamic schools has marginalized madrasas in the lives of middle- and upper-class citizens, who can now seek the best of secular, Western-style education and excel as professionals while maintaining their religious identities.[17]

Public high school education is the norm in Pakistan, and less than 5 percent of tenth-grade graduates study in private high schools. At this stage, it is unclear the extent to which Islamic schools in Pakistan will grow to be like the Darul-Huda in India to grant high school, college, and university diplomas and degrees. Between 2007 and 2008, I found at least five schools in Karachi, three under Shiite and two under Sunni madrasa alumni-operated administration, that continued on to the intermediate (grades 11 and 12) level.[18] Usually, students who go to these schools continue on to their affiliated Islamic intermediate colleges, where they take all subjects necessary to pass the nationwide grades 11 and 12 exams, with Islamic education added at the same level. This requires that families be able to afford private high school/college education in order to keep children in the same Islamic environment and to continue their education and upbringing in the same sectarian tradition. These high school/intermediate private Islamic institutions attached to Islamic schools are witnessing high enrollment. For example, Raza Ali, the administrator at the Shiite intermediate college that is part of a Shiite Islamic school near the Lyari area, a lower- to middle-income area of Karachi, informed me that between 2005 and 2008, the enrollment in his college had steadily risen five times.[19] Such enrollment shows that at least larger Islamic school establishments might eventually become full-fledged intermediate certificate granting (high school diploma) institutions. Unlike the Darul-Huda in India, no adult madrasa currently imparts degrees in secular subjects, and no public or private secular university has added a compulsory traditional Islamic educational program in Pakistan. However, since the state requires at least a Master's degree for those who teach at the university level, it will take much standardization of curriculum in preparation for both nationwide exams on secular subjects and Islamiat and standardization of the madrasa curriculum to meet state requirements before more Islamic schools become grades 1–10 institutions.

Recently, Robert Hefner and Muhammad Qasim Zaman have produced a collection of essays that discuss private Islamic schooling in various countries.[20] The authors highlight the fact that people's historical engagement with madrasa education as the sole repository of Islamic religious traditions is now changing in countries such as Egypt, Turkey, Morocco, Mali, Indonesia, and Britain as they are incorporating modern education with traditional Islamic instruction to produce modern, professional subjectivities in the students. It is possible that in the next decade, this type of Islamic schooling will not only marginalize the traditional, seminary-style of madrasa schooling but also become the modern definition of madrasa education. Therefore, it is important that more systematic studies be conducted on this blend of secular and Islamic education. To study the phenomenon, it is crucial for anthropologists to critically engage with everyday experiences of tradition, modernity, secularism, and class in the educational domain and to learn how people are creating and recreating traditions in response to their particular colonial histories and state policies.

The global Islamic schooling trend seems to point to a Renaissance-like return to classic authorities in Islam: the Quran and the *hadith*. Where social, economic, and political factors vary in each variety in this educational trend, the trend shows that people are not simply moving toward a classic puritanism that defies all later traditions. Rather, these educational reform movements are in reaction and resistance to a long tradition of puritanical madrasa education. In the case of South Asia, when all religious and social classes were competing to attract the attention of British colonialists, Darul Uloom Deoband was established by the Islamic revivalist Deobandi movement in 1866 to present a unified Muslim front in India in the face of the colonialists. Similarly, with the colonial master gone and the state continuing with a mix of modern colonial and modern local secular education, madrasas maintained their hegemony in these countries as parallel institutions of learning, where resistance to reform became equated with preserving ancient religious traditions. The enemy of the patrons of modern Islamic schools then became those who cherished this tradition, challenged its diverse interpretations, and resisted modernizing it in the face of changing social and global demands. Islamic schools are purifying Islamic traditions to basic Quran and *hadith*, similar to the efforts of the Deobandis, but they are also opening up Islamic traditions to critique from civil society and building a non-antagonistic relationship with the state, while remaining independent of its political designs and policies in relation to faith and education. This global reform movement through Islamic schools is what I would term *secularization*. Unlike the Western Enlightenment, this secularization does not represent a need to disconnect from and marginalize religion to create a modern society, but rather to make Islamic traditions, their interpretations, and systems of education more responsive to and encompassing of secular and modern realities. Such an engagement with secular ideals automatically breaks down the binary between tradition and modernity and reveals modernity as not a monolithic configuration emerging out of the West, but a pluralistic idea informed by varied engagements with tradition.

In the following section, I highlight the ways in which the existing body of anthropological literature on Islam, tradition, modernity, secularism, Muslim women's subjectivity, class, and Islamic education have influenced my approach in examining Islamic schools and the theoretical gaps I have attempted to fill through my own fieldwork.

2. Theoretical Implications of the Modern Islamic Schooling Phenomenon

In July 2004, I was standing at an Islamic bookstore in a Shiite middle-class neighborhood of Karachi browsing through material on religious education. I saw a man pick up a Quran textbook from the shelf. I asked him for whom he was buying it. He said that it was his son's school textbook. I asked him if his son went to a madrasa. Mr. Adil, as he later introduced himself, replied, "My child goes to a different kind of madrasa," and, when I asked for details about the madrasa, he corrected me saying, "It's a private school just like any other school, but O-levels, so no typical madrasa business and it's all high-quality, foreign, English-medium system, you know."[21] Mr. Adil, who along with three brothers runs a thread factory, is among the many upper-middle-class citizens who are not sending their children to madrasas but instead are patronizing Islamic schools. The kind of schooling that parents like Mr. Adil are promoting complement Islamic education with class concerns and use Islamic instruction as a means of legitimizing modern, Western-style education. In this section, I will discuss some of the important theoretical approaches that have helped me conceptualize the Islamic schooling being promoted by fathers like Mr. Adil.

2a) Conceptualizing Islamic Tradition, Secularism, and Modernity

To understand how the majority of moderate Pakistani Muslims understand the role of Islam in education, I attempt to break away from the dichotomy of Islam versus modernity and approach the reconceptualization of Islam following Talal Asad's approach.

> If one wants to write an anthropology of Islam one should begin, as Muslims do, from the concept of a discursive tradition that includes and relates itself to the founding texts of the Quran and the *hadith*. Islam is neither a distinctive social structure nor a heterogeneous collection of beliefs, artifacts, customs, and morals. It is a tradition . . . An Islamic discursive tradition is simply a tradition of Muslim discourse that addresses itself to conceptions of the Islamic past and future, with reference to a particular Islamic practice in the present. Clearly, not everything Muslims say and do belongs to an Islamic discursive tradition. Nor is an Islamic tradition in this sense necessarily imitative of what was done in the past. For even where traditional practices appear to the anthropologist to be imitative of what has gone before, it will be the practitioners' conceptions of what is apt performance, and of how the past is related to present practices, that will be crucial for tradition, not the apparent repetition of an old form.[22]

Samira Haj contrasts Asad's view of tradition with the traditional (i.e., the set of texts and practices that inform every new tradition).[23] The way "traditional" is defined by people according to the social conditions, practices, and arguments of a modern life transforms the traditional into the modern. The sectarian, ethnic, political differences, and class hierarchies signified by the people associated with these schools are ways in which people use past traditions, or *the traditional* corpus of Islamic knowledge that Haj points to, to construct a new tradition, which incorporates their discourses on professional needs, ethnic, sectarian, and political interests, and prestige concerns.

In the fifteen Islamic schools I examined in Karachi, some followed the Islamic code of conduct more strictly than others. However, administrators, teachers, and parents in all such schools admonished me not to confuse Islamic schools with madrasas, a word that connotes hatred and violence.[24] Qari Mohammad, owner and principal of two Islamic schools in North Nazimabad, a middle-class neighborhood of Karachi, invited me to his office during break time. Keeping one eye on the children playing, he said,

> We do not need to blindly follow the West to become modern. Islam *is* modern. We just need to understand that times have changed. This [Musharraf] government's reform agenda is not going to change anything. This O-level has also been followed from 1947. Did any of this change the situation that we are in? People have to find their own solution to religious extremism and learn from the good things of the Western tradition by educating themselves and . . . , he lifted his arms and opened his palms flat in front of me, "by balance . . . an Islam that comes from here," he pointed to his heart, "*and* here," he said, pointing to his head.[25]

Islamic school administrators like Qari Mohammad are using traditional Islamic education to form a new discourse of Islamic tradition in which extremism, violence, and ignorance of Western-based modern knowledge are erased, making space for a new form of modern education that neither replicates the colonial model of education nor reiterates the Musharraf government's "reform agenda" for traditional Islamic schooling.

John L. Esposito uses the term "Islamization" to understand the compatibility of religious tradition and modernity.[26] According to him, "Islamization" is the synthesis that emerges as a result of modernization going through a cultural filter to become acceptable. He conceptualizes Islamization as *both* local resistance to *and* the accommodation of modernization. Esposito suggests that Islamization should be considered as a coalition between the modern and traditional discourses.

As Qari Mohammad's discussion highlights, he wishes that people would respond to religious extremism and government crackdowns on traditional religious education by bringing, in Esposito's term, a form of Islamization that balances modernity and reason with Islamic tradition and faith.

Very often, the Islamization defined by Esposito is instead referred to by the term "Islam," as opposed to "Islamic tradition," the term used by the Islamic school administrators. In the context of finding a definition of modernity that is religiously and culturally viable and redefining Islamic tradition in ways that are less rigid, Islamic school-associated administration, teachers, and parents often say that they are looking for *just Islam*. At an Islamic school located in Nazimabad, a middle-class residential area of Karachi, for several consecutive days I asked the female teachers to arrange for me to meet with the principal, Mr. Hashmi. When I finally got an appointment with him, he began describing his school's effort to bring back the new generation to the basics of a peaceful Islamic way of life. I urged him to tell me more about the school's sectarian orientations. He became angry.

> See . . . that's what I am telling you! There's no *madhab* [sect] or *maslak* [synonym] here. Just Islam. The Islam that was revealed to Prophet Muhammad and that existed before people came up with all these sectarian divisions, which have ruined the reputation of our religious schools today and of our country. We don't teach Islam the conventional way. We just teach children how to understand and read Quran and know the founding principles of their *din* [religion] and you can see, I can show the textbooks to you, we teach all secular subjects like other schools.[27]

In the course of the next few months, I heard many alimat and administrators at Islamic schools describing their pedagogies as "just Islam." Pernilla Ouis says that during her fieldwork in the Arabian Gulf she noticed that, "A reference to Islam is gaining more legitimacy and credibility than a reference to traditions alone and can be used to reject certain traditions. Examples from fieldwork reveal that Islam is cited in the process of accommodating social changes in the Gulf."[28] Mr. Hashmi insisted that by not seeing Islamic tradition through the sectarian lens, his school has broken away from the madrasa version of Islamic education.

However, some Islamic schools, established by the madrasa alumni, are puritanical and follow a sect-based curriculum of Islamic instruction. As I elaborate in chapter 5, these schools do not teach a radical curriculum like the sect-sensitive madrasas and allow the students to engage in Islamic education using their cognitive and analytical capabilities. Rather, the school administrators and teachers develop sectarian subjectivities by acknowledging Pakistan's mixed religious heritage and controversial topics such as evolution in their curriculum and through what Giroux refers to as "the hidden curriculum," that is, the actual pedagogical process in class as opposed to the prescribed curriculum.[29]

Edward Said's *Orientalism* pushed scholars to examine Islam's position in relation to modernity in less ethnocentric and more critical ways.[30] However, the modernity of Islam was still viewed in terms of how closely it conformed to Western cultural and institutional arrangements.[31] In the wake of the formation of radical Islamist movements in the Middle East, scholars such as Emmanuel Sivan, Gilles Kepel, Jessica Stern, and others examined the political and ideological worldview of Muslims, but their studies remained confined to the extremists.[32] I argue that if levels of orthodoxy and extremity in religious interpretation and practice can be examined by considering the most extreme on the highest point and the most liberal on the lowest level of the chart, the scholars have adopted a top-down approach by focusing only on the extremists. Such a top-down approach does not lend agency to the majority of practicing Muslims and how they perceive their faith in a modern social environment and as politically active citizens. I asked twenty Karachi parents why they chose private Islamic education for their children. Each of them expressed distrust of the rhetoric of traditional madrasa *ulema* (scholars) to rally people's support against government checks on their activities and such. Moreover, parents expressed sorrow and concern at how traditional institutions of Islamic learning in Pakistan were being mocked by the international community.[33] Examining their responses, I adopt a bottom-up approach to understanding how Karachiites are configuring their relationship with Islamic tradition and education in the face of their modern, urban lives.

Samira Haj points out that Western definitions of the modern, which have long informed much of the scholarship on Islam, presume a necessary qualitative break with the traditional past.[34] The modern becomes the site of a progressive, emancipatory historical unfolding, in contrast to Islamic tradition, which is seen as a source of tyrannical politics and social suppression. Such an approach assumes that modernity cannot be experienced unless religion is marginalized from civil society, state, and politics. As Haj notes, such categorizations "do not adequately comprehend Islamic imaginaries or the forms of subjectivities that might possibly emerge in a modern Muslim world."[35] Describing this dichotomy of modern, secular and religious, outdated in Pakistan, Jamal Malik states that in countries such as Pakistan, which achieved independence from colonial rule in the mid-nineteenth century, state leaders internalized this Western notion of tradition and modernity.[36] The state manifested itself as the harbinger of modern education of the style that Western colonialists implemented in India after labeling the traditional system as unprogressive. Thus, a two-pronged attitude was adopted toward the traditional institutions of Islamic learning. While the state was ashamed to integrate traditional institutions into the public education system, the graduates of which would have the skills to fill blue- and white-collar jobs and contribute to the country's economy, it continued to let madrasas fill the need for education and room and board, unmonitored, for the masses deprived of public education. Every government has had a different policy regarding these parallel, informal institutions of Islamic learning. Where military regimes have patronized them to foster what is popularly known in Pakistan as the mullah-military alliance, or the politicization and radicalization of religion to justify martial law, madrasas' have lost the trust of the masses. Malik calls this state meddling the "colonization" of traditional Islamic education. Based on my own fieldwork, I attempt to take Malik's argument further by highlighting how, in the post-9/11 political environment, modern Pakistanis are using the private Islamic mode of schooling as a means to counter the state's colonization of traditional Islamic education and in an effort to disassociate traditional Islamic education from extremism, while ensuring that such an education prepares the youth to compete in the job market.

In Pakistan, madrasa education is usually associated with students doing rote Quranic memorization and blindly following the orders of strict teachers who tell them how to read and think about Islamic texts. This sort of education does not prepare students to participate in modern debates on ideology, professional growth, and politics.[37] By contrast, the unifying factor in the different types of Islamic schools I visited in Karachi is that they all teach Islamiat including studies on the Quran, *hadith* (sources on Prophet Muhammad's actions and words), and *sunna* (Prophet Muhammad's life). These subjects are taught by madrasa graduates. However, their content is not subject to the discretion of the teacher. The subject is codified similar to other subjects in textbooks accessible to everyone and is examined and revised by the administration and the parents. Moreover, Islamiat is not taught in Arabic as it would be in the madrasa, which further erases the necessity to hold allegiance to any religious hierarchy to understand Islam.

Inside the madrasas, Islamic learning happens from dawn to dusk. In the Islamic schools, it happens during regular class periods similar to other secular subjects. Any study on Islamic practice and education must take into regard this pedagogical outlook that constructs an alternative understanding of the process of Islamic education. Islamic school students first understand the Quran before reading and memorizing it. In a school opened by Sunni entrepreneurs in the middle-class area of Gulshan-e-Iqbal, I sat in on the eighth-grade Islamiat period, in which the chapter examined the place of music in Islam. The students first read the text, and then the instructor, Maulana Ashraf, asked them to tell him which parts of the text were understandable and which were not. Those who understood certain parts were then asked, one by one, to share their explanations, and then the teacher explained the difficult parts. The last fifteen minutes of the class meeting were reserved for miscellaneous questions, such as, "What is permissible media engagement in Islam and to what purposes should it be put?"[38] Dale F. Eickelman notes how people in conditions of modernity objectify religion, that is, define it as a holistic entity not subject to traditional authority and interpretable by anyone. Questions such as, "What is my religion, how is it important to my life, and how do my beliefs guide my conduct" allow people to redefine Islamic tradition and open it to newer conceptualizations.[39] Islamic schools, such as the one mentioned above, are replacing the hegemony that theologians such as Maulana Ashraf may otherwise have over Islamic education in the madrasas by an active engagement with Islamic knowledge. While attempting to revive traditional Islamic knowledge, the schools are also democratizing it and allowing the students to conceptualize it based on their own intellect. The transformed class environment in these schools also throws light on how, unlike the Western experience, Pakistanis are breaking the dichotomy of religion versus reason by modernizing and bringing critical engagement into traditional religious learning.

Mehnaz, mother of two boys and one girl who go to an Islamic school in the upper-middle-class area PECHS, said, "Don't think that the schools are brainwashing us into believing a certain interpretation of

Islam. The teachers teach everything from the syllabus and the textbook is updated every year." She showed me the back cover of an Islamiat textbook she was holding. "See, it says next to the logo. 'Approved by the Sindh Education Ministry!'" she read out loud and continued,

> The parents actually know what kind of Islamiat is being taught to the students. At the beginning of the year circulars are distributed to the parents about how much will be covered and in what way. If they do not agree with something, they can talk to the administration. There's no secret type of education going on here.

She shared a wink, hoping that I understood the implication on madrasa education. "And the standard of education is a lot higher than that in public schools."[40] Islamic schools, in this way, seem to be modernizing traditional Islamic education by discarding the authority of religious scholars and making Islam a "public property." Mehnaz conceives of the schools as conduits of Islamic knowledge rather than the institutionalizers of religion. She is among the many Karachiites who are interested in creating religious subjectivities in their children through a quality, private mode of schooling that is moral but critical.

Asad and Khalid Masud argue that the idea that a society undergoes secularization with the development of freedom of thought and increased human rights and political participation is only based on the Western experience of the Enlightenment.[41] Olivier Roy endorses this argument by stating that in order to understand new forms of religiosity in Muslim societies, we must revisit the concept of secularization.[42] The Western concept of secularism is equated with the absence of religion. Roy insists that this idea must be rethought when analyzing non-Western countries. He states that

> secularization is clearly a societal process; that is, it affects a society deeply, although it cannot be assigned to any particular level of that society (the economy, sociology, the role of intellectuals, and so on). It is the way a society looks at the world that changes . . . [Such] secularization automatically brings about a redefinition of religious adhesion.[43]

Roy's argument is useful for my examination of how, by supporting the secularizing of traditional Islamic education of the madrasas through Western education, Pakistanis are experiencing a form of secularization within the domain of religion. According to Roy, this form of secularization leads to "the obligation to define oneself explicitly as a believer . . . not because the nonbeliever campaigns against the religious community but because the conditions for belonging to the religious group have become stricter."[44] Similarly, the patronization of the private Islamic system of education seems to be an effort by modern Pakistanis to revive Islamic tradition in the country in an alternative to the method used in madrasas.[45] The form of religiosity that the Islamic school communities seek to promote must not mistakenly be called neo-fundamentalist because, although the Karachi parents who seek this form of schooling are, in Roy's terms, "born-agains," similar to the neo-fundamentalists, they are not against modern, secular education like the madrasa patrons. The school patrons seek to redefine Islamic education that simultaneously conforms to national educational policies. By contrast, madrasa patrons oppose government policies and are often interested in dismantling the government, securing political power, and establishing a theocracy.[46]

Patronizing private Islamic education gives Pakistani urbanites an alternative to the state's interpretation of Islamic practice and education. Zia's Islamization in the 1980s stemmed from a form of religious extremism in the country that the Musharraf government in 2002 decided to deal with by sacking the madrasas that stood as the ancient symbols of Islamic intellectual and spiritual glory for the people. I argue that the patronization of Islamic schools is a revival of religious sentiment that is "occurring against a background of secularization. It is an expression not of the persistence of religion but of a reorganization of the religious phenomenon according to patterns no longer operating within the traditional framework of the church-state pair."[47] The private Islamic schooling trend is an expression of urban citizens' secular experience, which they place between the state-defined Islam and the radical, madrasa-interpreted Islam.

Walter Armbrust, in his study of mass media in Egypt, observes that, unlike in the West, where modernity marks a break from past conventions and traditions, in Egypt modernity provides new contexts and vocabularies to maintain continuity with the older traditions.[48] In Pakistan as well, the emergence of Islamic schools represents one way in which some Pakistanis are incorporating their religious traditions within modernity and how secular education need not necessarily lead to marginalization of religious belief. Hirschkind, for his part, observes that "tradition-cultivated modes of perception and appraisal not only co-exist within the space of the modern, but are even enabled in ways by the very conditions that constitute modernity."[49] Borrowing Hirschkind's approach, I argue that the Islamic schooling phenomenon must be examined as the mode through which Pakistani urbanites challenge the assumption that modern education is a feature of secular modernity only. Joining the morning assembly at an Islamic school in Karachi, the sight that struck me the most was that *ulema* and alimat (female religious scholars) of Islamiat, *nazira*, and other Islamic subjects stood side by side with teachers for secular subjects. Being a product of one of the private secular schools in Karachi, the sight redefined the educational environment of a private school for me. A decade ago, except for some community-based schools for religious minorities, the presence of madrasa graduates along with graduates from secular public and private universities was irrelevant to private education and negatively affected the prestige of private schools. The Islamic school education, in this way, has ushered new ways of imagining secular and religious spaces. To endorse Armbrust's and Hirschkind's arguments, Islamic school entrepreneurs are reviving traditional Islam as much as redefining it by bringing together secular institution-trained teachers, who symbolize private/modern/secular schooling and madrasa-trained teachers, who symbolize traditional/religious schooling.

2b) Women, Modernity, and Islamic Tradition

The modern engagement with Islamic tradition in Islamic schools translates into their owners, teachers, and students observing the purdah, a form of religiosity which, according to Saba Mahmood, is problematic for modern feminist analysts to reconcile with modernity because, "On the one hand, women are seen to assert their presence in previously male-defined sphere while, on the other hand, the very idioms they use to enter these arenas are grounded in discourses that have historically secured their subordination to feminine virtues, such as shyness, modesty and humility."[50] In the 1960s, women's participation in such ways would have been labeled as "false consciousness" and "internalization of patriarchal norms."[51] However, studies conducted in the 1970s and onward paid attention to how human agency operates within structures of domination and "how women resist the dominant male order by subverting the hegemonic meanings of cultural practices and redeploying them for their 'own interests and agendas.'"[52] Mahmood adds to these studies by further arguing that Muslim women's practices in non-Western cultures should not simply be seen within the binary of resistance and submission to patriarchy, because such a binary presupposes women as suppressed or else experiencing agency through resistance only. Rather, Mahmood suggests that women's actions in the domain of religious observances should be seen as an alternative expression of religious behavior. The women that I spoke to inside and outside Islamic schools engaged and debated their religious tradition as much as the men. When female teachers, staff, and students wear scarves inside Islamic schools, they may be acquiescing to the dominant parental and patriarchal social norms, but they are also re-inscribing alternative forms of power that are rooted in a larger role in the job market and in the public sphere. As I observed in the Karachi Islamic schools, a phenomenon that I shall discuss in chapter 5, women are using the morality and legitimacy symbolized by this schooling system to increase their role in the public sphere.

An overwhelming majority of single girls sit home waiting to get married after receiving BA and MA degrees. These girls, and even those who are working before marriage, give up any ambitions of working after marriage. Young female teachers whom I spoke to in Islamic schools said that even after having made a family, when women decide to teach at the primary and secondary level, one of the most common and legitimate jobs for a woman, they have often been out of the field too long to find good jobs. Thus, many single female teachers whom I spoke to are working in Islamic schools to build work experience so that they can find jobs at better paying schools in the future.

While it is true when considering cases in which veiling has been used for female oppression and other political agendas, it is important to note that not all forms of veiling are oppressive. The Islamic schoolteachers whom I spoke to appear to actively engage with issues of modernity, morality, and modesty, rather than accept them as patriarchal norms. Mahmood examines the piety movement inside four mosques of Cairo and points out how women, through their increased activities inside the mosques, have virtually revolutionized their social environment.[53] Although the activities have radically transformed the lifestyles of these women, they do not see them as a successful social mobilization to trample the state authority or to campaign on their behalf as a disciplining force. Mahmood states that women's attempts to revive basic Islamic practice and morality in their lives must be understood neither as compliance to the state policies nor as resistance to the state, but instead as an alternative mode of religious practice. In Pakistan as well, private Islamic schooling represents an alternate educational tradition that seeks to define modernity and religion in accordance with the prevailing socioeconomic needs and political conditions.

Sitting with a group of female teachers at a Sunni madrasa-alumni-operated Islamic school in Bahadurabad, an upper-middle-class neighborhood of Karachi, I was discussing the principle of veiling with the English teacher, Ms. Safia, and how she thought the teachers were coping with it. Ms. Safia said,

> Don't think of the veil in these schools as something that you have to do. If anything is forced on you, you do the opposite of it. When we come to teach here, nobody tells us that veiling is compulsory to enter the school or anything. They only encourage it. If we feel like wearing an *abaya* [cloak] in addition to a scarf, we can. If we don't, nobody forces us. When I first took on the veil, I didn't know whether I liked it or not. Slowly, I felt secure and powerful in it. Now no one has to tell me to put it on. It has just become a part of me. I feel shame if I don't veil.[54]

Shumaila, who teaches science at the school, looked at me reassuringly and told me that she herself had seen Safia transform and that, in terms of her opinions and socializing, she is still the same colleague she was. She added,

> If you go out of this school, you'll find many other women who are veiled. Have you seen how they put it on, though? They wear seductive makeup, have the abaya stitched so tight and with so many slits that you wonder why they even wear it. This happens because they are not doing it out of their own will. It's not the veil that makes you pious.

There's the veiling of eyes and the veiling of speech also. If you don't train your eyes and mouth for modesty, no veil can make you pious.[55]

The story of Safia's spiritual transformation highlights a different engagement with Islamic modesty. Whereas secular scholars regard modesty as a human virtue, they see veiling as external to expressions of modesty. Teachers such as Safia, who adopt the veil, disassociate the practice from gender subordination. I adopt Mahmood's approach to veiling as an alternative religious expression in critical engagement with modernity to understand the narratives of Islamic school teachers who are using the school systems and its moral environment to redefine modernity in terms of physical appearance and also to increase their role in the public sphere.

2c) Understanding Islamic Education

Western literature on religious education in Pakistan usually revolves around madrasas and their relation to religious fundamentalism.[56] Such an approach identifies modern education with secularism and religious education with traditionalism. The analyses usually ignore the ways in which many Pakistanis conceive of their identities as balanced between Islamic traditions and modernity and fail to notice how different forms of religious schooling operate to create different religious subjectivities.

The literature on education produced by social scientists, journalists, and educational development centers in Pakistan is not confined to madrasa education alone. However, literature, largely in the form of reports and opinion pieces and the approach toward examining education in all such studies, is mainly reform-oriented.[57] The studies are based on comparative, statistical data or a comparative study of curricula in public, private, and madrasa school systems, in which schooling is assumed as a neutral process. Any pedagogical inquiry in these studies has been reduced to the analysis of how international and national funds are being allotted and distributed. The schools are presented as sites to educate a citizenry with good values, and the only actor is the state, which is evaluated for how its policies have affected the intellectual and economic condition of the schools. Although state policies, politics, and neglect are important factors in analyzing the educational choices of middle- and upper-class Pakistani urbanites, these analyses ignore the human agency and the diverse purposes of the people who establish them, who teach in them, and who send their children to them. The literature, therefore, overlooks systematic ethnographic descriptions of the various kinds of subjectivities that people who patronize particular forms of schooling seek to create. Local studies on Pakistan's education have yet to benefit from the advancement in critical education theory to analyze the politics of schooling.[58] By presenting my fieldwork on the diverse pedagogical strategies in Islamic schools, I attempt to cover this gap in the educational literature on Pakistan. In addition, I attempt to broaden the scope of Western literature on religious education in Pakistan by writing about an alternative religious education system rather than about the madrasas.

One anthropological study of education that I find useful for examining the private Islamic schooling phenomenon in Pakistan is Gregory Starrett's study of mass education in Egypt.[59] Starrett describes how the government uses religious education as a means of social control through the processes of "functionalization," which are "processes of translation in which intellectual objects from one discourse come to serve the strategic or utilitarian ends of another discourse. This translation not only places intellectual objects in new fields of significance, but also radically shifts the meaning of their initial context."[60] Starrett states that this functionalization is a strategy by which the Egyptian state in its race to "progress" puts Islam consciously to work for its own social and political projects and to legitimize its authority and control in the public arena.

Since Islamic schools are not state-created, I examine their emergence by linking the process of functionalization of religious knowledge to the agency of Pakistan's urban citizens. In a survey, I asked ten parents who were sending their children to these schools the difference between the Islamiat taught there and in private secular schools. Seven were of the opinion that Islamiat in private secular schools gives an inadequate, simplified, and shallow understanding of Islam and that real, in-depth, and traditional Islamic knowledge is provided by the madrasas. Yet these parents preferred Islamic schools over madrasas because madrasas provide minimal secular education and are too extreme in their interpretation of Islam.[61] Pakistanis are thus using their agency to patronize Islamic schools as a means to *functionalize*

Islamic tradition in ways that can enable them to obtain traditional Islamic education that is deeper than that offered at private secular schools, allows them to avoid the conservative outlook of the madrasas, and enables them to continue seeking the Western O-level education.

Malika Zeghal examines how modernizing reforms of the Al-Azhar University in Egypt in the 1950s and 1960s were an attempt by the Nasserist regime to control the ulema and undermine the religious basis of the institution.[62] However, by the 1970s, the ulema became "powerful political brokers," and religious education underwent a revival. Zeghal's work is important in that it shows how the state's education policies can backfire. In the case of Pakistan, when the Musharraf government announced its support for the Bush government's War on Terror in 2002, it cracked down on the madrasas and began inspecting their curricula and pedagogies. The effort led madrasa alumni to establish Islamic schools in all urban centers of Pakistan, including Karachi. The citizens, on the other hand, responded to the persecution of their traditional Islamic institutions of learning by choosing private Islamic instead of private secular forms of schooling for their children.

Zeghal's and Starrett's works are limited in providing guidance on these schools because they link the politics of religious education to the state rather than analyze how pedagogical processes are negotiated by the aspirations of the school entrepreneurs, teachers, students, and parents. The authors are not alone in this neglect, for, according to Bradley Levinson, "methodologically and ethically . . . schools are difficult places to study."[63] Educational anthropologists "assume, rather unanthropologically, that Western-style schooling has the same effects everywhere."[64] I attempt to use my field notes to highlight the political context, state policies, and social concerns that lead people to choose private Islamic schooling and how Islamic, sectarian, class, ethnic, and political ideologies are functionalized in the daily life of the schools.

2d) Toward Conceptualizing an Islamic Class Education

Since the 1960s, educational anthropologists have stressed that the schooling process cannot be understood as the process of communicating neutral knowledge. Instead, they have underscored how schools operate to disseminate preselected knowledge that maintains racial, class, and ethnic inequalities.[65] Ogbu, for instance, stressed the difference between the social reality of the schooling process and the experiential reality of schooling, that is, the inequalities and hierarchies that schools recreate.[66] Islamic schools present a case in point, as they represent both a revival of Islamic tradition in Pakistan and maintain the class inequalities promoted by private schooling. Following Ogbu, I attempt to present the social and the experiential reality of private Islamic schooling through the narratives of staff, administrators, students, and parents.

Drawing from fieldwork in Hammertown, England, with students from working-class families, Willis points out that inequalities created through schooling are not simply a result of the school's hegemony.[67] Rather, by creating a subculture within the school, opting for selective interaction and other activities that are distinctly working-class, working-class students deliberately reproduce working-class identities. Similarly, in the Pakistani Islamic schools, where the Islamic virtues of equality and humility are taught, students simultaneously acquire a distinct sense of where they are positioned in the social hierarchy. The upper-class families, usually from army and naval background, send their children to Islamic schools located in naval and army residential communities, where they may interact with students from similar familial backgrounds. In this way, these families endorse Willis's argument by deliberately using the schooling process to recreate their class identities.

Willis's argument, however, falls short of explaining the ways in which middle-class Karachiites are recreating their class status through religious schooling. Out of twelve parents that I spoke to outside three Islamic schools in the posh, upper-class residential areas of Karachi, eight lived in middle-class areas and preferred not to send their children close to home.[68] One such parent is Mr. Imran; he and his wife have two boys who go to an Islamic school in Defense, an upper-middle- to upper-class area of Karachi, rather than to one in Gulistan-e-Jauhar, a middle-class residential neighborhood where Mr. Imran and his family live in his parents' house. "We're saving up money and, *inshallah*, we'll move to Defense in five years' time. All teachers and students that come here [the Defense school], live in Defense . . . so it's good. Our children will learn how to move in that society before we do!"

I asked him if he thought Defense was good for the moral upbringing of his children. He said, "Yeah. It's kind of loose in Defense. No praying no nothing scene. Too Western sometimes. But that's why we chose to send our children to this school." He mused at his own comment, then waved a fist in the air. "It's a good way to keep them under control."[69]

Mr. Imran's story takes Willis's argument in a new direction, for Mr. Imran is neither trying to recreate the middle-class status of his children nor wishing for a linear ascendance to upper-class status. While economically and socially he wants his children to identify with the upper class, he simultaneously wants to inculcate in them a different moral worldview so that they do not grow up with religious values different from those of their middle-class parents.

Thus, while visiting Islamic schools and interviewing administrators, teachers, students, and their parents, I sought to understand how their "hidden curriculum" of these schools may create class subjectivities. Taking a lead from Giroux, I adopt the radical critical view to understanding their "hidden curriculum," which recognizes the relationship between economic and cultural reproduction and stresses relationships among the theory, ideology, and social practice of learning.[70]

The private Islamic schooling in Pakistan, offering the colonial O-level system, blends people's favored prestige education with the Pakistani religious traditions. Herrera points out that Western scholars usually regard Muslim societies' engagement with secular education in orientalist ways, that is, they assume that European-modeled schooling has been passively adopted by the people.[71] She highlights two flaws in this approach. First, the approach fails to observe how people adopt Western-based secular education in practice. Second, it assumes that the adoption of European schooling leads to the marginalization of religion in Muslim societies. In Pakistan, the madrasa system of education has co-existed with the British O-level education in private secular schools since 1947. However, it was the radicalization of their curriculum that encouraged Pakistanis to revive the traditional Islamic education of India in ways that would complement the colonial, O-level education. As parents like Mr. Imran break away from the private secular school O-level system and moving toward the private Islamic O-level system, they are using their agency to synthesize European education with their moral cultures rather than passively adopting it. Thus, far from becoming marginalized, the religious environment inside Islamic schools lends credibility to Western education. Anthropologists such as Arlene MacLeod, who recently described veiling practice among Egyptian working-class women as a mode by which social elevation and prestige is achieved, have examined the implications of Islamic practice for modernity.[72] However, such ethnographic studies on Islam have related class interests to Islamic practice but not to Islamic education. In educational anthropology as well, much ethnographic literature has been produced about class identities and subjectivities in schools, but none, including Herrera's study on the Egyptian Islamic schools, have examined the relation of Islamic education with class identities.[73] My intent here is to bridge the gap between the anthropology of Islam and educational anthropology by examining the class concerns of Karachiites in the domain of Islamic education.

In response to whether he approves of the private secular schools' educational style, Maulana Muneeb-ur-Rehman, a Sunni scholar and mufti (Sunni scholar and expert in Islamic law) who runs his own network of madrasas in Pakistan and is a prominent guest in religious discussions on local TV channels, remarked,

> In Islam, there's no concept of class. When everyone is equal, then their obligation to seek excellence in the teachings of Islam is also equal. It is important to seek other forms of knowledge, as the Prophet Muḥammad himself instructed us to do. However, a lot of times we treat Islamic education in a superficial way; we think we have learned all if we know how to pray or recite some *suras* [Quranic chapters]. Islamic education must be primary to every individual's life, no matter what economic class they belong to. If one puts Islamic education on the back burner, one is designating it as socially insignificant and then we don't pursue it as deeply as other forms of education because we think it is not as important. When we are so concerned about finding the best school for quality education and undergoing specializations to excel in other subjects, why have we subjected Islamic education for others to pursue?"[74]

Maulana Muneeb-ur-Rehman's opinion points to the missions of middle- and upper-class citizens, who promote private Islamic schooling to engage in theological training otherwise primarily restricted to the lower classes, by combining free madrasa education with private, privileged education, thus lending prestige and class to traditional Islamic education and making the idea of O-level style, secular education compatible with seminary education.

Pierre Bourdieu proposes new ways of understanding culture and class. He argues that culture is a form of capital similar to economic capital.[75] Cultural capital varies with the types and the extent of prestige in a culture. According to him, higher economic capital is significant to the construction of class and also to higher cultural capital. The extent to which the prestige or economic capital is higher depends upon the profession, the people defining it, the mood of the time, and the field (i.e., the social setting in which the capital is being conceptualized and sought). Elaborating on social capital, Bourdieu states, "The social fields vary in the particular forms of culture that pay off, but, in each field, the relevant forms are selected from the overall cultural hierarchy in ways that favor the dominant people in the field."[76] I asked thirty parents, twenty-one males and nine females, whose children went to various Islamic schools in four towns of Karachi, why they chose Islamic schools over private secular schools. All parents mentioned that the school had the O-level system and that the atmosphere in the Islamic school was religious. Twenty-six of these parents added that the tuition and other expenses for O-level education at Islamic schools were far lower than what they would have to pay at private secular schools.[77] Based on the parents' responses, I use Bourdieu's argument to propose that Karachiites patronize private Islamic education as a field through which an investment can be made to gain the cultural capital of British O-level education and Montessori pre-primary education alongside traditional Islamic education within the framework of economically prestigious, private education, signified by amenities such as computer labs, air-conditioned rooms, day-care systems, and so forth.

O-level education is a mark of class for the elite, but it is a mode of class elevation for middle-class families. Eqbal Ahmad points out that Third World and South Asian countries that continued a relationship with twentieth-century colonialists did so to benefit socially and economically.[78] A British education became a symbol of social distinction for the middle classes, who used the privatization boom in the country during the 1980s to spread the colonial label of education to secure well-paying white-collar jobs. In today's urban Pakistan, private Islamic schooling defines its cultural and economic capital by providing quality private schooling to middle- and lower-middle classes and passes on an Islamic cultural tradition that meets the sectarian, ethnic, and political interests of the citizens.

Conclusion

At an Islamic school opened by the Sunni politico-religious party Jamaat-e-Islami in a middle-class neighborhood of Karachi, I asked the administrator, Ishtiaquddin, why the trend of private Islamic education is growing in the country.

> For centuries, we had this form of education in our madrasas. Nowadays, they enter our institutions of religious learning, open our textbooks to see what we are teaching, and portray Islamic education on TV as if it is a faulted education, nauzubillah [We seek refuge in Allah from evil]. In our school, you can see how we are not ashamed of showing what a blessing Islamic education is for the youth, however modern we become and whatever are the needs of the time.[79]

Where madrasas symbolized Muslim presence during the British colonization of undivided India, the investigation into madrasa teaching after the September 11, 2001, attacks has encouraged citizens like Ishtiaquddin to experiment with private Islamic schooling, similar to the trend adopted in Indonesia, Egypt, and India.

I interviewed Tawfiq Islami, a Bangladeshi scholar, on an academic visit to Pakistan in Karachi. Islamic schools are also spreading in Bangladesh, imparting Islamic education with Bengali as the medium of instruction. "Because English is also prestigious in Bangladesh, these Islamic schools are only popular at the district level and amongst lower-middle-class families, while middle and upper classes prefer English medium secular private schools."[80] The growth of Islamic schools in India, Pakistan, and Bangladesh represents an important shift from traditional madrasa education to an Islamic education incorporated into modern secular education in South Asia. In this chapter, I attempted to situate this educational phenomenon in Pakistan within its broader trend and the theoretical implications of educational practice that redefine and mediate the issues of Islamic tradition, modernity, and class concerns. I attempted to point out the existing body of anthropological literature on Islamic tradition, modernity, Islamic education, and class and the gaps within this literature that my examination of private Islamic schooling phenomenon fills.

CHAPTER 3

The Educational System in Pakistan and the Place of Islamic Schooling

In this chapter, I explore the reasons why middle- and upper-class families are moving toward the private Islamic mode of education. I first examine the three main schooling systems in Pakistan—public/government, private secular, and madrasas—in the light of their historical development and political and social importance from the country's birth in 1947 to the time of the proliferation of Islamic schools in the last decade. Next, I examine the changing policies of the state regarding Islamic practice and education and how this has led to experiments with the style of religious education in the country and to the popularity of Islamic schools among middle and upper classes. Finally, I explore the socioeconomic reasons for citizens choosing this form of education.

The Education System of Pakistan

Education in Pakistan is divided into the primary level, grades 1–5; middle level, grades 6–8; secondary level, grades 9–10, after which students receive the secondary school certificate; intermediate level, grades 11–12, after which students receive a higher secondary school certificate; and university level, which includes the two-year Bachelor's program at an intermediate college, the three-year university undergraduate Bachelor of Honors program, the one-year Master's program, and the post-graduate program.[1] In 1947, there were three kinds of schools: the madrasas, the private secular schools, and the public schools. The public schools, private secular schools, and the new parochial private schools are from primary to secondary (grades 1–10) level. Madrasas, however, are institutions that may provide education above tenth grade.

All academic educational institutions are the responsibility of the four provincial governments. Karachi's institutions thus fall under the Sindh Provincial Ministry of Education.[2] The federal government is responsible for assisting in curriculum development and accreditation and providing some research funds.

1. Public Schools

Public schools teach secular subjects, such as math, science, social studies, English, Urdu, and Islamiat, required by the Ministry of Education. Public education is a sector much ignored by the government. Despite critical studies from international organizations as well as local education leaders in the country, the state has failed to make public schooling widely accessible for a fast-growing population or to bring quality to the existing schools.[3] Until democracy returned in 2008, the government budget allocation for education remained less than 3 percent.[4] Therefore, the quality of education in public schools, with a few exceptions in large cities, is poor. A high percentage of the schools do not have drinking water, toilets, playgrounds, furniture, electricity, proper structures, and, in many cases, even boundary walls. Thousands of government schools are "ghost schools," existing on paper only. Thousands of "ghost" teachers have been drawing salaries by simply showing up on pay day.[5]

Public schools were the preferred and affordable form of education for middle- and lower-class families until the 1980s, when lack of government funding and oversight led them to choose private secular schools. Whereas Urdu is the medium of instruction in public schools, English is largely a requirement for white-collar jobs. This has led over 95 percent of middle- and upper-class families to choose private schooling, to ensure their children's success in the job market.[6] Even the Education Sector Reforms, built on the 1998–2010 Education Policy, recognize the importance of establishing government standards for private-sector education, for their participation is necessary to provide an adequate number of schools for all children.[7]

Education in Pakistan and the Place of Islamic Schooling • 51

2. *Madrasas*

Since 1947, both public and the private schools in Pakistan have remained secular until the recent appearance of parochial schools. Madrasas have existed as parallel institutions of Islamic learning. They are supported by the government through a religious endowment known as waqf. These not-for-profit religious centers are run by four Islamic boards known as Wafaq/Tanzeem ul Madaris or Rabit-ul-Madaris. Three of the boards belong to the Sunni sects, which the majority of Pakistanis follow, represented by the Deobandi, Barelvi, and Ahl al-Hadith subsects, in order of dominance.[8] The fourth board represents the Shia minority.

Madrasa schooling is divided into the Dakhil (primary), Alim (middle to high), Fazil (higher secondary), and Kamil (college and post-graduate) stages. The concentration of religious teachings increases with each level. The core religious curriculum focuses on *hadith*, *fiqh* (jurisprudence), *tafsir*, *sunna* (Prophet Muhammad's actions), tajwid (chant illation), *sirat rasul Allah* (biography of the prophet), Quranic grammar, *aqaid-e-Islam* (beliefs) philosophy, and the like.[9] *Hafiz al-Quran* (the one who memorizes the Quran fully) or *qari* (the one who can recite the Quran with good pronunciation and in a melodic tone) are produced at the lower levels. The higher levels produce *alim*. The academic stature of a madrasa *alim* is equal to an MA degree holder in Islamic studies or Arabic from a regular university. A madrasa student, after graduating from tenth grade, has enough qualification to declare *fatwas* (religious edicts). Since few madrasas supplement religious education with secular subjects, the students who enroll in madrasas full-time do so with the knowledge that they will become well-versed in religious studies only and will be required to find jobs in the religious educational sector.[10]

All madrasas are required to affiliate with one of the four Islamic boards. The Islamic boards, in turn, are supervised by the Higher Education Commission (HEC) of Pakistan, a government organization established with the aim of making the country's universities world-class centers of education, research, and development. In order for a madrasa degree to become equivalent to an MA in Arabic or Islamic studies from a public (secular) university for the purpose of teaching Arabic and Islamic Studies in colleges and universities or for pursuing higher studies, the degree-awarding madrasa must be registered with the HEC.[11]

All Sunni madrasas grant a *sanad* (degree) to their graduates. Sunni madrasas stay open seven days a week. When I visited a Shiite madrasa in Karachi, a teacher named Sadaf described how the Shiite madrasa structure contrasts with the Sunni madrasa system: "You just study for fourteen years after which, if you want to further pursue theological studies, you have to go to Iran, in particular Qom, the largest religious center in Iran from where Khomeini began his revolutionary propaganda. Studying in a big madrasa in Iran promotes one to the level of *alim-e-deen* [scholar of the faith]," she said. Since no degree is granted and secular education is not emphasized, a child who has studied in a Shiite madrasa has to first clear the national matriculation exams before entering a college. After fourteen years, if a child does not pursue studies in Iran, he is made a helper or an assistant teacher and after four or five years, a permanent teacher. Shiite madrasas do not stay open seven days a week but only two or three days a week.[12]

As public schools are not accessible to the vast majority of lower-class families in the country, they turn to madrasas for basic education, because they also provide free schoolbooks, food, housing, and, in some cases, even a stipend. In addition, intense provincial and international migration toward Karachi has created some of the world's largest slum populations.[13] The blue-collar newcomers heavily rely on the madrasas to provide shelter, food, clothing, and basic education. This has allowed the madrasa sector to grow explosive rate.[14] Given the government's half-hearted reform efforts in the public education sector, these unregulated madrasas also contribute to Karachi's climate of lawlessness, by way of violent clashes between rival militant groups and the use of the pulpit to spread calls for sectarian and Jihadi violence.[15]

The majority of the madrasas in Pakistan emphasize rote memorization and encourage little critical thinking.[16] The teaching style of a typical teacher, especially in lower grades, is autocratic, and severe corporal punishment for not conforming to the rules and regulations is the norm. This also results in high drop-out rates in the middle classes; however, maids working in middle-class houses don't often have the choice to leave their children anywhere else.[17] Not only is there the strict regimen, but students have little idea of what is going on in the world outside. To ask questions is to act above one's station, thereby challenging the statuses of both listener and speaker.[18] Due to awareness of their low-class status, madrasa students listen to the *imam* and do not ask questions.

Pakistani madrasas today still teach from many of the Dars-e-Nizami texts. These are some of the oldest existing Arabic books, used in the medieval age and prescribed later by Mullah Nizamuddin Sehalvi in the middle of the eighteenth century. After his name, the traditional madrasa curriculum is called Dar-e-Nizami. The oldest books are in Arabic, then books in Arabic with explanations in Persian, and the most modern texts contain explanations in Urdu. Tariq Rehman notes the following regarding textual and language use in the madrasas:

> The Arabic books are treatises on grammar in rhymed couplets. One of the best known among them, Kafia Ibne-Malik, is so obscure that it is always taught through a commentary called the Sharah Ibn-e-Aqil. The commentary is often the dread of students and a source of pride for the teacher who has mastered it. In the madrasas, Arabic is not taught as a living language. The student is made to memorize the rhymed couplets from the ancient texts as well as their explanations. As the explanations in a number of texts are in Persian, which is also memorized, the student generally fails to apply his knowledge to the living language. Some ancient texts, such as the Mizbah-ul-Nahv, are explained in Urdu. But in this case the Urdu is very Arabicized. The explanation is scholastic and would not be understood, let alone convince, somebody who is not familiar with (and convinced by) the special branch of medieval Islamic philosophy on which it is based.[19]

Students in the majority of madrasas memorize the Quran without knowing that the Arabic they are reading is considered the hegemonic language of Islam. In the madrasas I visited in Karachi, similar to boarding schools, students stayed inside the madrasas and navigated outside in groups only for the purpose of missionizing and collecting private funds, thus interacting only with students from other madrasas. This system was followed by both primary and post-intermediate level students. Because of the lack of training in secular subjects, the majority of madrasa graduates cannot find jobs in nonreligious spheres. Therefore, they finish their education to become an *imam* (head of the mosque prayer) or to teach the Quran in the evenings at the homes of upper- and middle-class families.

While some madrasas aim to provide the same level of education as Pakistan's more elite schools, many offer only rudimentary training in science and mathematics. Many of the madrasas have built extremely close ties with radical militant groups, both inside and outside of Pakistan.[20]

At a madrasa that has separate branches for males and females in the upper-middle-class neighborhood of PECHS, I asked a male teacher, Maulana Saad Shabani, if his students read the newspaper. He handed over the madrasa's weekly newspaper to me. Major headline news from last week was compiled in there. I asked why the newspaper shouldn't be read in addition to the madrasas' weekly one. He said, "We do not want the students to develop a political ideology and corrupt their minds as it can lead to trouble."[21]

Pakistani madrasas tend to employ their own graduates. In the Sunni madrasas, a few teachers may also be graduates sent from the Al Azhar University in Cairo, one of the most ancient centers of Islamic learning to teach higher classes. In the case of Shiite madrasas, madrasa graduates who have gone to Iran to receive Islamic scholarship in Shiite *madhab* and *fiqh*, become ulema who guide the students.

In general, and before the proliferation of Islamic schools in particular, middle- and upper-class families who want their children to receive Islamic education send them to private secular schools during the day and to madrasas for supplemental Quranic lessons after school. Students from such families, therefore, do not reside in the madrasas and may or may not reflect their ideology after class. In essence, madrasas with their limited curriculum and pedagogical styles are not the primary or long-term educational choice for middle- and upper-class urbanites who aspire for their children to become good Muslims as well as to succeed in the job market.

2a) Mosque Schools

The rise of mosque schools has further diverted middle- and upper-class citizens from public schools. Religious schooling in the form of madrasas existed informally and parallel to the public schools until, in the mid-1980s, Zia-ul-Haq's military regime embarked upon a futile attempt to integrate the informal and formal education systems by opening up mosque primary schools, or primary schools that operate inside the mosques.[22] The plan, designed to compensate for inadequate public schools, was to add some additional subjects, such as basic Urdu and mathematics, along with studies in basic Quran and Islamic rituals and practices. The local *imam* (teacher) was to teach the subjects.[23] Twelve thousand mosque schools were opened.[24] The plan faced serious challenges, as many of the local imams had never received formal schooling and were not academically prepared to teach Urdu and math. Many mosque schools closed soon after opening, while others survived to impart limited Islamic and no secular education.[25]

The democratic government that succeeded General Zia-ul-Haq's martial law under Benazir Bhutto had little interest in the mosque schools. Prime Minister Nawaz Sharif's government that followed, however, promoted Islam's role in social life and education. The government reverted to Zia-ul-Haq's policy of using mosque schools to compensate for the lack of public schools. The National Educational Policy of 1992, therefore, announced that 107,000 new primary and mosque schools would be set up to ensure universal primary education to all citizens.[26] The Education Policy of 1998–2010, promulgated by another military regime, that of General Musharraf, reinforces the idea of setting up mosque schools along with public primary schools to provide adequate provisions for free schooling. The plan has the strategy detailed in table 3.1:[27]

The above table shows that, even though the Musharraf government cracked down on madrasas, the government continued to rely on mosque schools to provide basic, free schooling to the public. Data sources conflict in the exact number and functional status of these schools. In 1998, a source estimated there to be more than 25,000 mosque primary schools operative in the country. In 2007, the *Daily*

Table 3.1 Education Policy: 1998–2010

Facilities/Services	*Benchmark 1996–97*	*9th Plan Targets 2000–2003*	*Policy Targets*
New Formal Primary Schools	145,000	162,000 (+17000)	190,000 (+45,000)
Mosque Schools	37,000	40,000 (+3,000)	57,000 (+27,000)

Times reported them to be as few as 5,000.[28] Like the madrasas, these schools are also supported through government endowment (*waqf*). The reduced number highlights desperate efforts made by the Musharraf government during protests against the martial law to incorporate mosque schools into public primary (grades 1–5) schools in order to monitor them and ensure that they impart both religious and secular education.

Similar to the public schools, the mosque schools suffer from a lack of facilities and have an outdated religious curriculum, pedagogical style, and no training in secular subjects, similar to the madrasas. It is not a coincidence that private secular schools have remained the primary schooling choice for middle- and upper-class families since the Islamization of education in the 1980s.

3. Private Secular Schools

Private education in Pakistan has a long history pre-dating independence. In a country in which 50 percent of the population is under seventeen years of age, private schools are the primary means of quality education. They are regulated by provincial education boards, which are in turn supervised by the Federal Education Board of Pakistan.[29] The schools independently decide tuition fees and textbooks and hold internal exams up to eighth grade.

From 1947 to 1980, there were a handful of costly private schools—missionary-run schools or local schools that imitated the missionary model and only catered to the Pakistani elite. These schools offered the national and/or the British education curriculum, the latter having a higher prestige value.[30] In the 1970s, Pakistan had a severe balance-of-payments deficit. The government, under Zulfikar Ali Bhutto, encouraged both skilled and unskilled men to work in the Persian Gulf countries as a way of dealing with this deficit.[31] The construction boom in the Gulf states at that time provided Pakistani men with plenty of labor jobs, and, by the mid-1980s, with an estimated two million men, Pakistanis made up the largest group of foreign workers in the Gulf states. These men were remitting more than US$3 billion every year to their families at home.[32] Simultaneously in Pakistan, the privatization boom in the 1980s encouraged many entrepreneurs to open private secular schools. The remittances of Pakistani migrants allowed a greater number of middle-class families to send their children to private secular schools. Since the 1980s and until private Islamic schools emerged, private secular schools have been the primary schooling choice for the upper- and middle-class citizens.

Given the scarce number of quality public schools, the government relies heavily on private schools to meet educational needs. The government policy toward private schools is still laissez faire—there are no subsidies in the form of grants to parents or schools, so that private schools arise and survive purely as a market-based phenomenon.[33] Today, private secular schools range from those charging very low fees and located in one-bedroom apartments, to those in rented bungalows, to schools in proper buildings with campuses in all parts of the city. In the five private secular schools that I visited in Karachi, the fee ranged from Rs. 80 per month to Rs. 10,000 per month (roughly US$1–125). The schools on the higher end of the range were more prestigious and located in the posh areas of Karachi. Private schools have become an alternative for parents serious about educating their children, despite middle-class parents often experiencing extreme financial constraints to meet the tuition costs.

Some private secular schools were for either boys or girls only. Girls at certain times in a school day in some private secular schools would wear head scarves, but the pedagogies and code of conduct in all private secular schools, regardless of the ideological orientations of the entrepreneurs, remain secular. Unlike the madrasas, in which full-time students study from dawn to dusk and many live inside the madrasa, the private secular schools are open between 8:00 AM–3:00 PM and, therefore, the students have different social lives outside the schools. Secular subjects such as math, science, English, Urdu, social studies, and so forth are taught in private schools, according to the Ministry of Education guidelines, but with leeway in the choice of textbooks and manners of teaching art, music, and other extracurricular activities. The graduates of private schools join secular public or private intermediate colleges and universities and are geared toward finding white-collar jobs in the public and private sectors.

3a) Matric versus O-Level System
At the ninth- and tenth-grade level, some private schools may offer the national matriculation system, commonly referred to as the matric

system, which is followed in all public schools, or the British O-levels system, or both. O-level (ordinary level) system is a colonial system of modern education that Pakistan inherited. O-level subject-based qualification is conferred as part of the General Certificate of Education (GCE) and is administered through centers in Cambridge and Oxford, United Kingdom. England, Wales, and Northern Ireland replaced O-levels with General Certificate of Secondary Education (GCSE) exams in 1988. However, the O-level is still used in many Commonwealth countries, including Pakistan, where the system, because it is administered through and recognized in Britain, has a higher prestige level than the Matric system.

In the Matric system, education is completed in ten years, at the end of which students take nationwide examinations to proceed to intermediate college. In the O-level system, first- to tenth-grade education is completed in eleven years, at the end of which students appear in examinations conducted through the British Council–administered international GCE system in different cities of Pakistan. After completing O-levels, a student may go for A-level (advanced level) in the GCE system, which is equivalent to eleventh- and twelfth-grade public, intermediate colleges. These colleges are from grades 11–14; that is, they offer two years of high school education and two years of Bachelor's education, similar to community colleges in the United States. At these secular colleges, students can choose to do two-year Bachelor's programs in engineering sciences, medical sciences, or in arts. Some students also choose to complete tenth-grade Matric system education or O-level, eleventh and twelfth grades from intermediate colleges, or A-levels, and then enter Bachelor's and Master's programs at public and private universities. Many middle-class parents pay high tuition to graduate their children through the O-level examination system and choose cheaper intermediate colleges after tenth grade, instead of the handful of institutions offering A-levels. The foreignness of the O-level system represents higher English proficiency and larger access to white-collar jobs, as a result of which many private schools are replacing the Matric system with the O-level system to attract middle- and upper-class parents.[34]

All students who wish to take the Matric system exams, whether they are enrolled in public or private schools, are placed by their respective provincial ministries of education at various public and private schools that serve as examination centers.[35] By contrast, O-level students can take exams in any number and kind of subjects at the ninth- and tenth-grade level depending on their preparation level at their private schools.

In the tables below, I summarize the subjects taught from grades 1–8 and grades 9 and 10 (based on both the Matric and O-level systems) in public and private schools and madrasas.

In the public and private schools, social studies and science in grades 1–8 are replaced by Pakistan studies, physics, chemistry, and biology in grades 9 and 10. Islamiat is taught in both public and private schools as a codified subject, similar to the secular subjects. Non-Muslims have the choice of taking ethics instead of Islamiat from elementary school to the university level in Pakistan.[36] The British Council–conducted exams are based upon the curriculum set and administered by the Cambridge International Examinations, a major provider of international qualifications for students between the ages of fourteen and

Table 3.2 Review of Subjects Taught in Grades 1–8 in Public Schools, Private Schools, and Madrasas

Subjects	Public Schools	Private Schools	Madrasas
Science	Yes	Yes	No
History/Social Studies	Yes	Yes	No
Islamiat	Yes	Yes	Yes
Urdu	Yes	Yes	No
English	Yes	Yes	No

Table 3.3 Review of Subjects Taught in Grades 9 and 10 in Public Schools, Private Schools, and Madrasas

Subjects	Public Schools	Private Schools	Madrasas
Pakistan Studies	Yes	Yes	No
Biology	Yes	Yes	No
Physics	Yes	Yes	No
Chemistry	Yes	Yes	No
Islamiat	Yes	Yes	Yes
Hifz/Quranic memorization	No	No	Yes
Nazira/Quranic recitation	Yes	Yes	Yes
Urdu	Yes	Yes	No
English	Yes	Yes	No
Quranic Arabic	Yes	Yes	Yes

nineteen in more than 150 countries. For Pakistani candidates, Cambridge prepares Islamiat and Urdu papers. In this way, religion and national language, as well as modern secular education are all integrated into a foreign system that, because it is administered outside the country, falls outside the jurisdiction of the federal and provincial ministries of education in Pakistan.[37]

Because the medium of instruction at public schools is Urdu, Islamiat is, with a few exceptions, always taught in Urdu. The Islamic emphasis in the social studies curricula was first added under Zia-ul-Haq's martial law in the 1980s, to Islamize the country's educational structure. The Quran and Arabic subjects were later added in the same vein under Nawaz Sharif's second time as the prime minister.[38] Therefore, in public and private schools, curriculum it is not reflective of the school's ideology, but rather of the state's changing relationship with Islam's role in the social and educational lives of the citizens.

Ninth and tenth grade results in the Matric or the O-level exam system are crucial to obtaining admission in the very few and very expensive A-level institutions that charge approximately US$100–300 and above per month in tuition in addition to US$500 and more in admission fee (US$1 = Rs.100), or to get admission in the public intermediate colleges, where tuition is nominal, but the nationwide competition for admission is extreme. Only a handful of private colleges offer grades 11–14 education. Thus, the choice of primary and secondary schools is a crucial investment for middle-class parents, so that they can save on their children's education later. This quality education must stress high English proficiency, which is not possible through government/public schooling, where English is only a codified subject and not the medium of instruction, for access to white-collar jobs. Upper-class families, on the other hand, send their children overseas after they complete their O and A levels.

3b) English and the Importance of Private Schooling

Proficiency in English is the deciding factor for the educational choices of Pakistanis. In 1947, Urdu was recognized as the country's national language. English was adopted as the official language for the time being to make provisions for Urdu to replace English in that capacity. When General Ayub Khan imposed the first martial law in the country, he patronized English-medium private schools and established cadet college and convent schools across Pakistan. For the common folk, Urdu-medium schools were created. This attached a status symbol to English, as the Urdu-medium school students only graduated to work for small salaries under English-medium school graduates. In 1959, the Sharif Commission was formed, which said that, until Urdu was ready to replace English, English should continue to be used for advanced study.[39] This granted English another fifteen-year lease and maintained its prestige.

The 1973 Constitution of Pakistan, the country's present constitution, promulgated under Zulfikar Ali Bhutto, granted another fifteen-year lease to English.[40] Bhutto nationalized all schools, but, in the elite private schools, English continued to be used. As the champion of privatization, when General Zia-ul-Haq deposed Bhutto in a military coup, he denationalized all educational institutions, which not only resulted in a mushrooming of private schools all over the country, but also encouraged the entrepreneurs of the previously established private schools to switch the medium of instruction in their schools from Urdu to English. Simultaneously, Zia-ul-Haq's new National Education Policy of 1979 aimed at Islamization of the curriculum, which meant making Islamiat and Arabic mandatory in schools.[41] Urdu was to replace English as the medium of instruction in 450 schools countrywide. However, federal schools under defense and missionary control out-voted such transition. To add to the confusion, in 1983, the general allowed science subjects to be taught in English in the non-elitist government schools.[42] The democratic governments of Benazir Bhutto and Nawaz Sharif continued this parallel system of private English-medium and public Urdu-medium schools, a system continued by General Musharraf. Being the official language of Pakistan, English continues to be taught in public schools, but, in private schools, all secular subjects, and often even Islamiat, are taught in English.

The dubious state policies on private schooling and the significance of English for professional success explain Mateen's comments. Middle- and upper-class families sending children to private evening tuitions is a common urban culture in Pakistan. Tutoring becomes a substantial source of income for lower-middle-class educated youth trying to make ends meet. Mateen was a computer engineer I met who was offering private tuition in the evening to pay for his college education. He lived in a joined family system and had an ailing father to take care of. He recounted,

> However smart you are, however hardworking you are, nothing matters . . . go to an interview, talk in English, you'll get the job. It is really hard to grow up and learn it . . . it's not the same. I have a Master's in computer engineering and seven years of experience. I have seen my CV put on the side in front of computer diploma holders who know English. Rehan [his son, who goes to an Islamic school located in Gulshan-e-Iqbal, a middle-class area of Karachi] is lucky that he has our example. There was no one to guide us. Now I tell him to practice English even when he comes back from school and secure a good job . . . maybe he can get admission in UK or USA.[43]

For parents like Mateen, private English-medium schools are the connection to professional growth in private enterprises and the international market.

Having discussed the different school systems in Pakistan and the social prestige of English-medium education, I will now examine why Karachi parents are moving toward an Islamic form of private schooling.

4. Why Private Islamic Schools?

Why are middle- and upper-class parents choosing private Islamic over private secular schools? I will address the question in two ways. First, I will examine the relationship of the state's educational reforms and Islam in Pakistan to understand the political and social environment in which parents grew up, who are now choosing private Islamic schooling for their children. Next, I will look into the social, economic, and ideological reasons that are attracting urban parents toward this kind of schooling.

4a) State's Educational Reforms and Islamic Ideology of Pakistan

Disparate social and political actors, under the patronization of and in resistance to the state, have vied to use schools for different purposes. This has conditioned how Pakistanis perceive Islamic practice and education and underscored the need for the private Islamic system of education. In August 1947, Pakistan was created in response to the demands of many Muslims in colonial India for the creation of a Muslim majority state. Ever since, religious, secular, and socialist political parties continue to struggle over the nature of Islam's role in state affairs.[44] Two examples illustrate the nature of this struggle. President Bhutto (1971–77) started his rule by taking economic and political power from the military, feudal, and bureaucratic elites and handing it over to the middle and lower classes. Many religious parties, however, considered Bhutto's socialist and populist leanings constituting an atheistic affront to Islam.[45] Toward the end of his rule, Bhutto coined the term *Islamic socialism* in an attempt to win back the religious political parties. He tried to connect his policies with the Prophet Muhammad's teachings.[46]

In the 1973 Constitution of Pakistan, Bhutto included the declaration that Islam is the state religion and no law repugnant to Islam can be enforced in the country. Ahmadis are followers of a nineteenth-century Islamic religious movement based on scholar Mirza Ghulam Ahmad's teaching that are considered heretical by orthodox Muslims. Bhutto, under pressure of Islamic leaders, also enacted the legislation that designated the Ahmadia community as non-Muslims, prohibited them from attending Islamic rituals, and removed them from all positions of public service or office in the armed forces. Right before his overthrow by Zia and imposition of martial law in 1977, Bhutto went as far as banning alcohol, gambling, bars, nightclubs, and movie theaters.[47]

On the other hand, General Zia, who succeeded Bhutto, justified his imposition of martial law as a means of bringing about the "Islamization" of Pakistani society. All financial institutions were brought under Islamic principles of economy. Under the Hudood Ordinance, Islamic restrictions for Pakistani Muslims were laid down, which have prompted criticism by both domestic and international human and women's rights organizations. Islamization was also brought about in the dress code and curricula of public and private schools and universities. Under Zia, madrasas received the greatest state patronage in the history of Pakistan.[48]

Zia-ul-Haq's revitalization scheme was part of an effort to Islamize Pakistani laws, institutions, economy, and society. Politically, it meant producing Islamic militants, Jihadis, for the Afghanis' fight against the Soviet occupation.

In 1979, Zia gave madrasas and Darul Uloom the status equal to public and private schools. Under the Islamization policy, madrasa sanad was declared equivalent to a Master's degree in Arabic/Islamic studies given by a secular, public university. The Zia government, similar to the ones that came before, failed to provide a sustainable solution to the nation's high illiteracy rate. As madrasas, especially with post-1980s Islamization, grew in number, many operated, and many still do, without registration with the Higher Education Commission (HEC). After Zia, four democratic governments came and were removed from power until Musharraf staged another military coup in 1998. Musharraf needed the religious parties to bolster his military dictatorship against the democratic forces seeking to reverse his 1999 coup.[49] After the September 11, 2001, attacks, the link between Pakistan's religious education system and international terrorist organizations came under intense scrutiny by the Bush government's War on Terror, and the Musharraf government cracked down on madrasas under the policy known as "Enlightened Moderation."[50] On June 19, 2002, the federal cabinet approved the madrasa Registration Ordinance 2002, in force immediately, to regulate religious schools by bringing them under the formal educational system of the country. According to the ordinance, madrasas must register with the Pakistan Madrasa Education Board and its respective Provincial Madrasa Education Boards. Madrasas violating the ordinance risked closure, a fine, or both. The government also tried to persuade schools to teach science, mathematics, English, and Urdu so that madrasa graduates might eventually enroll in professional schools. It was also announced that madrasas would receive government aid only if they began providing what could be termed a "modern education."[51]

While the reform was welcomed by some madrasa ulema, its goal was to incorporate elementary English language skills, simple math problems, and some Urdu. The suspicion that incorporating any greater degree of modern education would take students' focus away from religious service, the lack of prepared faculty to teach these subjects, and the fact that going through highly difficult classic texts in the Dars-e-Nizami syllabus left little room to add other subjects to a degree that aimed to bring madrasa graduates on par with secular school graduates led some madrasa ulema to introduce some books, but only as window dressing.

Due to differences in quantitative data based on government, private, and informal sources, it is hard to estimate the number of madrasas that were registered. However, by January 2007, over 12,000 of Pakistan's estimated 13,000 madrasas had registered with authorities.[52] In practice, because of pressure from the clergy, the only penalty for not registering a madrasa was ineligibility to receive government funding.[53] From 2002 to the resignation of Musharraf in September 2008, the government maintained an ambiguous policy toward the madrasas. The radicals maintained their avenues for propagating militant ideas, because the chief patrons of jihad—the Jamiat Ulema-e-Islam and the Jamaat-e-Islami political parties—acquired prominent and powerful roles in Musharraf's political structure.[54] In this way, the government never fully implemented any program to register the madrasas, follow their financing, or control their curricula.[55] The dramatic army siege outside the Lal Masjid (Mosque) and its associated madrasa in July 2007, exhaustively covered by national and international media, was one of the most dramatic efforts toward realizing the missions of the Enlightened Moderation policy.[56] However, because religious parties continued to enjoy political power, the extremism could not be curbed, even after the military rule was overthrown by a civilian government in the 2008 elections. The result was the struggle of the democratic government of the Pakistan People's Party (2008–2012, whose founder was Zia's predecessor, Bhutto) to curb Taliban and other extremist organizations' violence in the country.

The same challenge awaits Nawaz Sharif's government (2013 to date, overthrown by Musharraf in 1998) after it received power from the first democratic government ever to complete its tenure in Pakistan. The radicalization of madrasas under martial laws and the instability of democratic governments are reasons why—contrary to the popular perception in the West about educational and religious educational choices of Pakistanis—middle and upper classes consider the madrasas as low prestige and scandalous institutions of learning.

4b) Popularity of Other Educational Experiments in the Face of State Policies
The social impact of Zia's Islamization, the resultant radicalization of the madrasas, and the Musharraf government's crackdown on madrasas has contributed to several experiments to incorporate Islamic learning

in everyday life in moderation. Below, I summarize some efforts in Islamic education that gained popularity among middle- and upper-class citizens during my fieldwork.

i.) The Guidance   During August 2007 to March 2008, administrators at only two out of seven madrasas I visited informed me that their response to the government has been positive and that they have incorporated subjects such as Urdu and math to modernize their curriculum to bring it on par with public and private schools.[57] However, the medium of instruction in these madrasas remains Urdu. As Mrs. Emaan, teacher at a madrasa told me during my visit, "English is the language of the West. With language comes the culture. So, there is no place for English in a madrasa."[58]

The Guidance Network of female madrasas emerged in the early 1990s and has gained widespread popularity among middle- and upper-class women in Karachi and other cities in the last two decades. These madrasas are not schools, but continuing education centers in which traditional and Sunni madrasa education is offered in English. The lectures are given using modern technology. Women are allowed to discuss Quranic ayat (verses). Whereas teachers already had marked portions in one or two Quranic commentaries to teach from in the madrasas I visited, at The Guidance madrasa branches I visited in Karachi, teachers include lectures on divorce, as well as teenage issues, such as dating, smoking, and so forth. On their official website, The Guidance calls itself an NGO (nongovernmental organization) encompassing education in Islamic morals and marriage counseling. The Guidance's teachings enable affluent women to discuss the effects of urban life on family structure and their children's life choices. It even provides marriage counseling. It transforms women from passive symbols of religious piety to active civil citizens. Shumaila, a woman in her thirties with a Master's degree who was working for a private news channel in Karachi, had begun attending The Guidance in the fall of 2007. Speaking to me, she contrasted her educational choice, The Guidance, with a traditional madrasa:

> Madrasas are just a refuge for the destitute where, once enrolled, the student stays for good . . . is kept socially isolated and then the next thing you know he's blowing himself up! I chose The Guidance because

unlike how we see in other madrasas, these people don't promote any madhab [school of thought within Sunni Islam] . . . of course it's Sunni . . . because that is the actual religion, you know . . . but just simple Islam. You are not tied to it all day. There are convenient summer courses, fast track courses for those who come with little or no knowledge, and two-year diploma courses. The teachers here are very aware.[59]

As Shumaila's statement highlights, The Guidance is a madrasa purely for urban Sunni women and girls. Its uniqueness lies in how it attracts independent, working, upper-middle-class women like Shumaila, who also intended to bring her two-year-old daughter to The Guidance for its children's program in the future. The Guidance madrasas have changed the image of madrasas by doing missionary work among the elite class. This also makes it attractive for women from lower-middle-class families who seek upward social mobilization by association with it. Shumaila used very little Urdu with me in her conversations and later explained that by saying, "The Guidance teachers are aware," meaning that they were educated and spoke civilized English.[60] Both the teachers and students at these madrasas are women who have graduated from private secular institutions. Even the least educated have an O-level certificate. Women need not have had an association with a madrasa as a child, and they can choose to enroll in the offered courses if it suits their work and family life or otherwise ask for a different course schedule. The Guidance madrasa is also attractive for working women like Shumaila because learning does not continue all day as is the case in other madrasas, so that once students leave the madrasa, they can work, study, and socialize in their own social circles.

Contrary to other madrasas, The Guidance branches are not attached to a mosque. The Guidance graduates I met conduct and attend their private sermons and group readings in Quran, *hadith*, *nazira*, and *hifz* at each other's houses. The network thus signifies a piety movement among elite and middle-class women. In advertisements, The Guidance offers summer camps along with Quran classes in English. The very idea caters to the middle and upper classes and ex-patriots visiting home. For people of such classes, invitation to join a religious institute should be as attractive as a summer camp.[61] By not constructing Islamic ethics in opposition to Western practices, The Guidance connotes modernity for urban women. The Quran classes are offered alongside personal grooming and nutrition/fitness.

The Guidance madrasa reaches out to women through cassettes and CDs which allow women to choose whether they prefer to receive religious instruction without formally joining or taking courses at The Guidance. Yet through these cassettes and CD sermons and discussions, women in increasing numbers are becoming active members of The Guidance community and agents of its brand of Islamic piety. Many women listen to The Guidance's message and begin courses on their own at home or by congregating in a designated international hotel chain in an upper- or middle-class neighborhood where they share The Guidance's teachings and learn from each other. The growing popularity of The Guidance, in particular in the post-2002 crackdown on the madrasas, represents another effort on the part of middle- and upper-class citizens to promote an alternative form of religious educational institution that does not connote militant religious extremism. The Guidance packages privileged, class-based madrasa-style education that meets people's changed gender roles and their urban lifestyles. However, it does not provide systematic secular education. Islamic schools, by including secular subjects from first to tenth grade and sometimes up to twelfth grade, are filling this void.

ii.) Reforms in the Private Secular School Examination System: The Case of Aga Khan University Examination Board Where alternative madrasas are trying to counter the need for modern Islamic education, some experiments have also been made to reconcile the dichotomy between the prestigious O-level and the local, Matric system in public and private secular schools. One such experiment has been the Aga Khan University Examination Board (AKU-EB) developed by the Aga Khani (Ismaili Shiite) establishment of Pakistan. It was formed to improve the curriculum and format of the ninth- and tenth-grade nationwide exams and assess students in their critical-thinking skills. During fieldwork in Karachi, I came across four Islamic schools and seven private secular schools (both Sunni and Shiite), that follow the local matriculation system and have affiliated themselves with AKU-EB.[62] AKU-EB allows private schools to completely disengage from the state system of evaluation. The board's Islamiat curriculum encourages students to ask questions about Islam and analyze various aspects of its teachings in relation to other religions. Parochial schools are choosing it as a way to induce religious tolerance and peace in their otherwise traditional madrasa curriculum. The Aga Khan Board is also working to increase concept-based evaluation in the local matriculation exams. If more English-medium private schools following the Matric system register under the AKU-EB, the prestige attached to the O-level examination system will diminish, which might lead to an increase in the ratio of parochial and private secular schools offering the affordable Matric system and decreased tuition costs.

iii.) Tuition Culture and the Quranic Schools   In all cities of Pakistan, there are private tuition centers, one or more on virtually every block offering evening lectures in secular subjects, most commonly English, math, physics, chemistry, and accounting for O-level, A-level, and generally for all students from ninth to fourteenth grades who are studying to take the nationwide, federal board exams. The centers are in high demand with students whose parents are illiterate, who have missed classes, whose schools lack quality instruction by highly qualified teachers, or who suffer from teacher neglect in overcrowded classrooms and offer packaged, fast-tracked revisions of the essential components, including science labs, of the curricula. In the last decade, some tuition centers have emerged offering crash courses in Quran and Arabic. In addition, Quranic schools, similar to the mosque schools established under the Zia government but not attached to mosques, have also proliferated, running as independent tuition centers and offering classes in mornings, afternoons, and evenings. The clientele of tuition centers that offer Quranic lessons are middle- and upper-class families who send their children to private secular schools and want to supplement the education with Quranic learning. Amir, a contractor by profession, sends his son, Hashim, to a private secular school in Clifton, a high-income area of Karachi, and on weekends to a Quranic school in the same area. He explained the reasons:

> You can set a personalized schedule with them based on your commitments. You can be sure that if you drop the child at two, he will

have a two-hour class, and then he is done. So, when the child is there, only class is happening. No madrasa-type feeding about extremism, or politics.[63]

I spoke to Haji Sami-ul-Haq, a Pakistani who lived in Egypt for several years and graduated from the Al-Azhar University. He told me that he teaches Arabic and Quran at three different tuition centers in Defense and PECHS, upper- and upper-middle-class areas of Karachi. He conducts separate classes for girls and boys and designs the courses according to the education level of the students and their prior level of Quranic reading and Arabic.

> Times have changed. Pakistanis, like I saw in the [Persian] Gulf, are realizing that being a true Muslim is about becoming independent possessors of Arabic, Quran and *hadith*, so as to better understand the manner in which the state interprets Islam and how it is described in the West.[64]

Religious learning was, until now, never a part of the tuition center culture of Pakistan. The objectified mode of Islamic education in the form of Quran and Arabic classes promoted by the tuition centers is a phenomenon that is transforming the concept of tuition culture in Pakistan. Whether Quranic lessons at tuition centers will become ways for Islamic school students to revise the Islamic education they receive in class is yet to be seen. However, the Quran schools represent the middle- and upper-class citizens who grew up under Zia's Islamization to train their children in the discipline, language, and literary tradition of Islam, such that they are not dependent on the authority of religious scholars like the madrasa students, but rather active agents of Islamic education.[65]

iv.) Digital Islamic Education Simultaneous to the crackdown is the increasingly popular trend among urban citizens of acquiring Islamic knowledge through digital sources. When I was visiting madrasas in Karachi during my fieldwork, I was often provided or instructed to listen to sermons and lectures by Islamic scholars on issues ranging from the fundamentals of Islam to controversial opinions concerning veiling and to debates over the influence of Western cultural values over Pakistani Muslims. Several other times, I heard religious sermons and debates in my informants' cars. When an informant of mine, Safia, a marketing consultant at a multinational corporation, got into her car and automatically popped in a CD sermon about gender issues in work environment on her way to the Cineplex for a business social night, I couldn't resist asking her why she did it. She first looked offended. When I explained that it was for my research, she articulated her thoughts patiently.

> You know we don't work nine to five . . . we work twenty-four hours . . . if you've left in the morning, come home at 10:00 PM, there's only time to eat and sleep . . . it is impossible to take time out for *dini talim* [religious education] . . . Nowadays, nobody has time. But then sometimes I pick up a newspaper or become part of a heated discussion with colleagues in the office about Muslims and Pakistan, religious terrorism and stuff . . . and I think that one cannot make an informed argument if one hasn't had any religious education . . . what is right, what is wrong . . . how will you debate, how will you defend your identity . . . so, I listen to the opinions of various scholars to debate in an attempt to not sound like the rest of the people [viz a viz] . . . cavemanish!"[66]

Examining Islamic revival in Cairo, Egypt, Hirschkind argues that listening to tapes of Islamic sermons induces a "moral state" that is articulated within the "traditions of Islamic self-discipline."[67] The digitized Islamic literature is allowing Pakistani citizens such as Safia, who are not formally trained in theology, to judge the stance of Islam in relation to modern debates on human rights, morality, and lifestyle on their own. In a group interview, I asked eight students from the University of Karachi what had emerged as a result of the Musharraf crackdown among the youth. The majority of the group spoke about an increased consciousness to participate in debates about Islam, and Internet blogs and debates were mentioned as the mode through which the students express their opinions on such issues. The cassette sermons and lectures of Pakistani and non-Pakistani religious scholars punctuate the lives of urban Pakistanis like Safia and link them to their religious traditions as they drive to work and run household chores. They serve as agents of self-improvement and evaluation in times when Pakistani madrasas are labeled by the Musharraf government and by domestic and international media as an unreliable mode of receiving moderate Islamic education. This form of Islamic instruction—which includes discussions on the challenges to Islamic practice in the modern age, the influence and consequences of Western cultural and religious values on Pakistani society, and other issues—punctuates the daily routines of many men and women and ushers in a nonviolent and conditioned Islamic revival that is in harmony with the social conditions of a modern, secular, and urban life.

Digital literature and the Internet in this way share the space with Islamic schooling in defining and extending the public space of religious discourse and contributing to the "massification of education in the contemporary Muslim world, which has given wider access both to the texts of Islam and to a wider range of interpretation than is developed in the mosque-university [madrasa]."[68]

v) The Private Islamic Schooling Experiment When the Musharraf government ordered madrasas to register with their respective madrasa boards, many madrasa administrators, to escape police scrutiny, changed their madrasas into Islamic schools. This became a strategy for a number of madrasas that did not want the government to control their curricula, pedagogies, and activities. In chapters 4 and 5, I categorize these Islamic schools as the puritanical, madrasa-alumni-operated Islamic schools. All private secular schools function under the provincial education boards that are in turn controlled by the Federal Education Board of Pakistan. The British O- and A-level system, however, is foreign, and therefore exempt from government scrutiny. By turning madrasas into private Islamic schools, the madrasa administrators avoided crackdowns and scrutiny, continued to function, and also received state patronage as private schools. Adopting the O-level system, which is controlled by the Cambridge and Oxford centers in the United Kingdom rather than the government of Pakistan, keeps administrators free of government checks on the examination system, syllabi, fee structure, and so forth. The private mode of education allows former madrasa administrators to receive the same state patronage extended to other private schools. Furthermore, the Ministry of Education does not impose a specific text or curricular guidelines for teaching Islamiat in private schools. The Islamic schools take advantage of this by adopting textbooks published by their own press or those that present secular subjects within an Islamic framework. In this way, they are able to integrate traditional style of Islamiat into the curricula without violating any regulations of the ministry.

The Karachi parents whom I interviewed, whose children attend Islamic schools, were between the ages of thirty-five and fifty and were, for the most part, raised during the era of Islamization. Soon after beginning my fieldwork, I visited government offices to meet people who could think through history with me. That is when I met retired Colonel Ehtesham, who now supervises the welfare and community unit of officers in a middle-class area of Karachi. Why are middle and upper classes shifting from private secular to private Islamic schools? How is their choice related to our political history? He told me that he would feel more comfortable taking up the discussion at his residence. This time, no code of conduct as in the madrasas ordained that I come with my father. However, Musharraf and the army were still in power, and thus it was hard to trust a colonel still linked to the army who had at the beginning of our conversation inquired: "Are you with some human rights watch? Some private channel news team? Why do we need to talk about Zia or President Musharraf?" and only believed that I was contextualizing schools for research after I explained my research for three hours. Therefore, I visited his residence with my father serving as guard. Colonel Ehtesham explained,

> People want to find balance. Look what our history has been . . . Bhutto comes with Communism, Zia brings Islam . . . you can't completely make people either overnight. Had the democratic governments done something to counter the spread of religious extremism and unsupervised madrasa education, maybe people would have found the balance. Now, we have a different military rule. They are rounding up madrasa people . . . teachers, students, supporters at the mosque . . . if you are a Muslim praying five times a day, such scenes look appalling . . . perhaps these private Islamic schools that you are looking at are the solution . . . the way to balance between the leftist and the rightest politics that affect the masses . . . people have nothing to do with you, I tell you . . . all people want is to make the best of the two worlds.[69]

Looking back at the way the state has experimented with Islamic ideology and the role of Islam in education and social life and the way the current government is also trying to balance and redefine in its own way the place of Islam in society, Colonel Ehtesham's explanation stayed with me.

The Musharraf government crackdown encouraged many moderate parents whom I met in Karachi, between the ages of thirty-five and fifty, to find a reliable educational solution. Nada, mother of three girls who go to the Read Islamic school in Karachi, spoke to me inside the school's admissions office.

> This is so shameful. We should be ashamed of ourselves. We are doing things in the name of religion that are causing such international humiliation for us. Where is education in all this? Should we then decide that Islam is bad? No, it is not. And we can prove it . . . I am not involved in politics so I won't comment about what is going on in the madrasas and on TV right now. Let the government and the un-Islamic madrasas do what they want. I chose this school, because English, science, et cetera type of education is important, but in our present scenario, it is also important for me to teach my kids the Islam I learned about at home. This school is moderate and suitable for that purpose.[70]

I interviewed a Jamaat-e-Islami activist, the late Mr. Khusro, at his residence in Gulshan-e-Iqbal, a middle-class neighborhood of Karachi, where he runs a Jamaat-e-Islami Islamic school. I asked him why now, after all these years—Mr. Khusro was in his eighties—he had decided to help establish a private Islamic school. He replied,

> This military government is no different from the British. The colonialists had tried to do the same by suppressing Islamic education in the subcontinent, but our ancestors established the Darul-Uloom Deoband madrasa in India to protect their Islamic tradition from fading away. Today, not only our own Pakistani state is putting a façade of liberalism by turning our madrasas into the state's pulpits but also giving a free ticket to the West to do whatever about them. We will not allow Western intrusion. We will also not allow the state to make madrasas a public mockery.[71]

Many madrasa administrators whom I spoke to during my pilot fieldwork in 2004 and 2005 said that the government's sudden U-turn policy to support the American war instead of supporting its own people had caused great disenchantment in the people. Therefore, "Government is the reason why radicalism will increase more forcefully than before," said Maulana Hafizur Rehman of a madrasa located in Gulshan-e-Iqbal, a middle-class neighborhood of Karachi.[72]

In both the resistive behavior of madrasas against the government ordinance and parents like Nada moving toward private Islamic schooling are suspicions of what the government describes as "reforms" in the traditional sector of Islamic education. While the mullahs/maulvis (religious teachers) have reacted to opposing government reforms, citizens are taking their children out of private secular schools and enrolling them in Islamic schools. The schools seem to meet a need on the part of the eighties generation to define their Islamic identities somewhere between Zia's state-imposed Islamization and Bhutto's socialistic modernity and to provide their children with a stable and moderate education. The Islamic school blend of secular and religious education seems to meet a need on the part of the eighties generation to solve the ideological deadlock of Pakistan and to define a position somewhere between state-imposed Islamization and socialistic modernity; public and private schools and madrasas are no longer adequate to fulfill this task.

In the following section, I discuss the social, economic, and ideological concerns that motivate Karachi parents to choose private Islamic over any other kind of schooling for their children.

4c) Social, Economic, and Ideological Aspirations for Choosing Private Islamic Schooling

Unlike the Islamic schools in Egypt, Islamic schools in Pakistan have not emerged as alternatives to state-controlled religious education.[73] Rather, they complement state curriculum requirements while simultaneously using the liberty of private schooling to add traditional madrasa curriculum. In the past, many parents who sent children to private secular schools chose to supplement secular education with religious knowledge, either by sending children after school for short-term courses in Islam at madrasas or by hiring a *maulvi* to give Quranic lessons at home. With the emergence of Islamic schools, parents have found a practical and economical mode of providing children with both secular and religious education from a single institution within school hours.

In Karachi, I asked fifteen parents why they chose to send children to Islamic schools. Ten replied to the effect that it was because the private secular schools, offering modern and O-level education, had become too Westernized. Parents feel that, even as the standard of O-level education in these schools is high, the dominance of Pakistani upper-class culture in the schools, represented in smoking, drug use, indulgence in pornography, psychological problems, dating, and intermixing of the opposite sexes has diverted children from their religious values and cultural traditions. Thus, more parents are opting for private Islamic schooling because it offers a quality British education system in an environment in which all learning, activities, modes of dress, and gender space comply with Islamic principles and Pakistani cultural values.

In one Islamic school that I visited in the upper-class area of Defense, the administrator told me that the school would soon start a daycare center in which parents could leave preschool children during working hours and their school-aged children after classes ended.[74] The daycare feature highlights how educational institutions are adapting to the changing social lives of Karachiites. As educated women increasingly work outside the home in schools, beauty parlors, and government offices, the demand for daycare facilities has risen. Hirschkind notes, "Tradition-cultivated modes of perception and appraisal not only co-exist within the space of the modern, but are even enabled in ways by the very conditions that constitute modernity."[75] Islamic schools provide the facilities and prestige of private (including Western) education while fulfilling the demands of a nuclear family. A parent, Mrs. Anila, spoke to me about what guided her choice for her son, Emad:

> I teach at the Bay View School [a private secular school] at Civil Lines [area bordering Clifton, a high-income area of Karachi], where the salary is decent compared to that in other schools. My son Emad is in an Islamic school Montessori in Clifton. Because he's still in pre-school, he gets off at noon. I get off at 2:30 PM, and by the time I get here facing traffic and all, it's already past 3:00. At first I wanted to enroll Emad where I teach. But the Montessori fee at my school is so high that all my salary was being spent on his Montessori training. So we thought that it's better to save for his primary and secondary education. A friend of mine told me that the Islamic schools are nice, the environment was Islamic, all the teachers were also decent and that they had daycare service. So I got Emad enrolled here and it's working out for me. They have a very reliable system. He takes lunch and they make sure that

he eats it after he gets off. They allow children to either sleep or play until the parents come. Daycare system is a necessary provision for our society. There's no other place to leave your children and many women are working nowadays.[76]

The emphasis in Emad's school on daycare facilities, along with the madrasa environment and secular education, highlight how Islamic schools are transforming the image of madrasa education; unlike traditional madrasas that discourage women's activities in the public sphere, Islamic schools such as Emad's, established by madrasa alumni, are facilitating life for working women.

Islamic schools are attractive for parents because they offer both religious and secular education during school hours. Quratulain, mother of ten-year-old Shoaib told me,

> As soon as my son comes back from school, I feed him and then instantly put him to bed. Then I wake him up after an hour and it is really hard for him to freshen up again, especially in hot days like today [it was October] with no electricity. He goes to madrasa and after coming back he instantly gets to his homework. You know how much homework the schools give. By the time it's done, it's close to midnight. If you send the kid to madrasa you and your child feel left out. Your kid cannot play with other kids after school. If there's a social gathering that you want to attend, you cannot. We prefer these [Islamic] schools because we want to give Islamic education that suits our routine.[77]

Another social concern of the Karachiites that private Islamic education meets is their desire for the English-medium, British O-level education that, to use Bourdieu's term, provides them the "cultural capital" to ensure success in the job market.[78] In Karachi, despite Islamic schools being present in upper-, upper, middle and lower-middle income areas and lower-middle income areas, parents from middle-class areas choose to send their children to Islamic schools in upper-class areas, so that their children socialize with students from upper-class families and acquire their mannerisms. Although many private secular schools offer the O-level system, the fact that Islamic schools legitimize Western education by imparting it in an Islamic environment has made the schools unique for parents who desire to simultaneously create moral, class, and modern subjectivities in their children.

Mark Liechty, in his study of middle-class culture in Kathmandu, observes that "the meaning and experience of modernity lies in a daily balancing of the demands and possibilities of a transforming social and material context against those odd and deeply rooted cultural milieu of moral values, systems of prestige, and notions of propriety."[79] Between August and November 2007, I conducted informal interviews with fifteen parents at six Islamic schools located in middle- and high-income areas of Karachi. To my question—"Why did you choose to send your child to a private Islamic school instead of a private secular school?"—eleven responded that private secular schools had become too Westernized. I asked if they were satisfied with the standard of O-level education in private secular schools and they responded in the affirmative. Ayesha, the mother of one eleven-year-old boy and a fourteen-year-old girl told me her story. "They used to go to Beacon House. They say it's O-level and there is no doubt that the education is good, but," Ayesha lowered her voice,

> the environment there is very out [of control] . . . kids throw cash around like crazy . . . after school, you can see them walking out the gate smoking and they even exchange drugs . . . their parents know it, but they are not involved . . . and the teachers cannot do anything, because the students and parents get angry at them . . . just the other day, a boy, a year older than Zara [the daughter] pulled a gun out of his pocket. Zara said that she has seen that many times. She has even seen boys distributing porn. The TV today, all uncensored channels, MTV and what not . . . kids copy all the Western stuff they watch on TV . . . all the action movies . . . kids in that school even go out on dates . . . tell me, is this our culture? Is this Pakistani culture? No, kids nowadays live here, but their minds are in America . . . can you ask kids today to pray? They talk back at you, but you tell them play video games, they are all up for it. I was seeing them go out of my control, so I moved them to this Islamic school.[80]

Beacon House is a private secular school, which attracts middle-class citizens because it is known for its English culture and English-medium teachers from upper-class areas. Ayesha's narrative was similar to those that I collected from fourteen other parents.[81] It shows two concerns: The encroachment of Western culture on Pakistani and Islamic cultures through media; and quality, O-level private secular schools such as Beacon House becoming agents of Westernization such that it is leading to the cultural and moral degeneration of Pakistani youth.

Asif, parent of a ten-year-old boy at an Islamic school in Gulshan-e-Iqbal, explained why he chose to send his son to an O-level Islamic school instead of an O-level private secular school. He pointed out,

> There is O-level here and there's no difference . . . nowadays, every school is O-level, so the quality is not any higher at a regular private school. But in addition, this school is safe . . . they tell children to dress modestly, they have character-developing activities, boys and girls are in separate classes and it's strictly English-medium. So, I feel good when I leave my son here in the morning. I know he won't come home with foreign values.[82]

Parents like Asif equate private secular schools with the kind of free society in which an absence of a religious moral code makes Western, modern education equal to disregard for one's own cultural and religious values. Like Asif, more parents are opting for private Islamic schooling because it offers a quality British education system in an environment where all instruction, school activities, modes of dress, and gendered space comply with Islamic principles and Pakistani cultural values.

Over the last two decades, inflation has made it increasingly difficult for many middle-class parents to pay school fees, and so many choose private schools based on affordability. The fees, quality of education, and prestige of each private secular school varies and creates a class hierarchy, for which middle-class parents invest their lifetime savings to pay high fees for schools located in upper-class neighborhoods. Such investment provides an avenue for social elevation and better prospects in the job market, where association with high-caliber English-medium schools gives a graduate an edge above graduates from smaller, private secular schools located in low-income neighborhoods. Islamic schools charge lower fees than private secular schools. In particular, Islamic schools that are jointly owned by madrasas become beneficiaries of donations and public and private endowments allocated to madrasas. They are, therefore, the most attractive for middle-class parents looking for affordable O-level education.

On August 11, 2007, one of the most humid days in Karachi, I was thrown out of an overloaded public bus by a multitude of elbows fighting for space. I had finally reached a Shiite Islamic school in PECHS, an upper-middle-class area of Karachi. Right at the gate, the school sign read many things, but, wiping sweat off my gasoline-layered face, I could only read one thing: "Air-conditioned!" I walked in along with several mothers and fathers holding their children's hands. As people sat on chairs lined up against the wall to talk about admissions, I caught several eyes staring at me. I didn't look like someone who was here to obtain admission for her child. "Here to teach?" guessed a woman next to me.

I explained what had brought me there and complained about the heat.

"Hmm . . . do you have light at home?" she inquired.

I mumbled an "I guess."

"Go home and I'm sure it's gone by now. We haven't had it for two weeks! Transformer fault. We have to get a school for him," she said pointing toward her son. "Couldn't get to it because I was waiting for my husband to come from the Gulf," she said pointing to her well-dressed husband. "He has also come to this misery, but his arrival doesn't help because he doesn't know what schools are out there."

"So what have you decided?" I asked.

"I don't know. He [her husband] and his mother say that it doesn't matter if the school isn't big enough. The environment should be decent. That's their only priority."

"And what do you think?" I asked.

She chuckled, pointing to the high-roofed admissions office. "So far, I've landed us in a decent environment. And they have air-conditioning here! Plus, with all the schools filling up fast, we might never get free admission elsewhere. I'm enrolling him, no question about it!"

If air-conditioning was all that appealed to the anthropologist in me, I totally agreed with her educational choice for her son. My number was announced before her, but she jumped ahead, knowing that I didn't need it as much as she did.[83]

Najia, who lives in an apartment in Federal B Area, a lower-middle to middle-class income area of Karachi, is one of the many Karachi parents who are coping with the lack of facilities in the government schools; the incapacity of the madrasas to train students for professional jobs, the religious norms of their families, and their budgets and in these circumstances are choosing private Islamic schooling.

During the course of my fieldwork, my conversations with at least sixteen parents mirrored Najia's comments about how the private schools provide certain luxuries and facilities and about how the scandals over maltreatment and lack of basic provisions in madrasas makes the Islamic school education seem like a better choice. I interviewed Qasim at an Islamic school located in Guru Mandir, a lower-middle- to middle-income area of Karachi. Qasim is a parent of two who works as a computer technician at an engineering firm with a monthly income of Rs. 6,000 (US$60) and is the third of five brothers. He lives with his parents, his wife, and two children, and the brothers' families in his family house. I asked him about what his educational priorities for his children, given his budget limits. He pointed toward the big sign at the school gate that read, "Free admission!"

> I have done a lot of running around trying to get computer diplomas for a decent job. This school has computer education at no extra charge. If my kids learn it from an early age, they won't have problems finding jobs later on. The tuition is cheaper than that in the private [secular] schools I surveyed and the school uses audio-visual equipment in teaching for which there is no additional charge.[84]

The biggest burden on middle- and lower-middle-class parents is the admission fee, ranging from Rs. 10–70,000 (approximately US$100–700) depending on the school's prestige, that they must pay in addition to monthly tuition, stationary, uniform, and contract transportation charges. With the information technology boom coming to Pakistan and other South Asian countries in the 1990s, employment avenues in the global telecommunication service sectors opened up for Pakistanis. This encouraged many schools to give computer training at the secondary level. In the ninth and tenth grades, corresponding to the British O-level, many schools began to add elective courses in computer studies.[85] Some madrasas continued to regard the computer as a satanic machine, while others, knowing that their clientele is predominantly poor, did not show interest in computer education. After the 2002 crackdown, many madrasas began establishing computer labs as a way of showing that they had incorporated secular education. However, it is unclear whether any teacher is formally employed to train students in the field.[86] Now many Islamic schools are offering computer education, which has created a new image of Islamic education for parents looking for spiritual and professional success for their children. For middle-class parents like Qasim, the free admission and computer education means valuable savings that can be invested in the family's health and housing needs. Thus, very often, the choice of Islamic education is simply an economic and professional one for middle- and lower-middle-class parents.

Islamic schools hold computer classes either every day or once a week. Sajida, a female social studies teacher at an Islamic school said to me,

> This school may be imparting Islamic education, but we are not opposed to the computer. If its use is supervised, it can serve as a good source of knowledge. There was a time when the Muslims ruled from Saudi Arabia to Spain. Why did they lose their power? Because the West adapted itself to new technology and the changing needs of the time. We can only compete with them if we do the same. That is what Sir Sayyid Ahmed Khan wanted the Muslims to do.[87]

Sir Sayyid Ahmed Khan was a nineteenth-century political thinker and scholar, who is deemed by Pakistanis as one of the first Muslims to work for the representation of the Indian Muslims under the British rule. After ousting the Muslim rule under the Mughals, the British remained suspicious of this minority community in India. The Muslims met this suspicion by boycotting the British educational and political system. Believing that the future of Muslims was threatened by the rigidity of their orthodox outlook, Sir Sayyid began promoting Western-style scientific education by founding modern schools and journals and organizing Muslim intellectuals. He upheld that learning English and Western-style education was the only means by which Muslims could come up to par with the colonialists. Interestingly, Ms. Sajida stressed the importance of computer education within an Islamic educational institution as a way of countering the West. She saw the role of her Islamic school as analogous to Sir Sayyid's role in awakening Indian Muslims to demand their rights from the British on an equal footing.

Private education, with English as the medium of instruction, is a mark of social superiority and class. Since the government sets no uniform standards for private schools, Islamic schools may offer the prestigious, British O-level education, but some, similar to the elite private secular schools, may own their own swimming pools, which is a luxury in Pakistan, while others may function inside one-bedroom apartments above bakeries and mattress stores. Islamic schools that cater to elite families of army, bureaucratic, and naval backgrounds are among the more prestigious. For example, elite Islamic schools set themselves apart from others by offering meal plans to the students, a chic and novel concept in private education. "Like the Americans do, you know," Asia, mother of a fifth grader at one such elite Islamic school, proudly told me. "You just pay the tuition expenses. The kids eat breakfast and lunch there and they even have their lockers and don't have to carry those heavy bags around and break their shoulders and backs."[88] This concept was new to me, because even the elite private secular schools that I had known did not do that. There are a few elite private secular boarding schools in Pakistan, which are largely established by the army to educate children in strict, cadet-like discipline. The Islamic school that the mother mentioned is unique because it has incorporated the meal-plan system of boarding schools into day schooling. As Asia described, it is optional to take the plan but hardly anyone opts out because the administration asks the parents not to send food from home so that the children learn how to eat whatever is cooked, share it with children coming from other backgrounds, and acquire training to live independently. To encourage children to live on their own from a young age is a unique feature of private Islamic schooling, because Pakistani children generally do not move out of their parents' houses upon adulthood, and male children may marry and nurture their own families in the same house they grew up in.

Mehnaz was another mother I met whose son was to appear in the O-level exams at the British Council, Karachi, as an elite Islamic school student. She encouraged the training saying, "Children in this way learn self-help and interact with others on an individual basis, which is important when they go to the States or to UK for higher education." Mehnaz's comment highlights how some parents use Islamic schools to provide an Islamic base to their children in hopes that their children will have a clear understanding of the code of conduct they will follow if they end up in a foreign (read Western) culture for professional reasons.

Conclusion

Discussing the issue of religious extremism in Pakistani madrasas, Robert Looney suggests that "Developing alternatives and supplements outside the formal educational system" is a good way to counter extremism.[89] Pakistani urbanites seem to be following along the lines of Looney's suggestion by promoting the private Islamic education system. However, Islamic school staff whom I spoke to in Karachi never used the word *madrasa* for their schools, so as to be considered as religious institutions operating like other private schools with the authorization of the provincial education ministry. Naeemullah, chief accountant at an Islamic school operated by the religious political party Jamaat-e-Islami in the middle-class area of Gulshan-e-Iqbal, Karachi, said,

> Everything we do is out in the open. If you want to check our accounts book, you can do so. We keep ourselves up-to-date about any changes to the curriculum and regulations issued by the Ministry of Education and even though the government doesn't do much to help us monetarily, we incorporate as many facilities as possible.[90]

According to P. W. Singer, madrasas are problematic institutions for three primary reasons: they promote school violence, challenge the state, and hurt economic prospects.[91] Conversations with parents, administrators, and teachers at Islamic schools in Karachi highlight that the popularity of these schools lies in the fact that their education is government-supervised, professionally promising, and based on an interpretation of Islam that creates modern religious subjectivities in the students. Islamic tradition in some of these schools, as I will describe in chapter 4, may be interpreted diversely though based on differences in the sectarian traditions and practices. However, the schools operate under government regulations and are not associated with breeding Islamic militants. In contrast to the madrasas, where students are evaluated through their respective sectarian madrasa boards, Islamic school students take the nationwide board examination system in ninth and tenth grades and in the few Islamic schools that have incorporated intermediate/high school education, students continue to take nationwide, public exams in the eleventh and twelfth grades. Their exams are graded just like those of students from other secular schools and intermediate colleges. Their compliance with the state laws makes them attractive for urban parents who want an education for their children that is scandal-free and safe.

A madrasa education creates economic depression, because madrasa graduates, receiving only religious education taught by rote memorization, are handicapped in the job market.[92] They do not have the intellectual skills to earn white-collar jobs with their sanad. The Islamic schools meet this challenge through modern science and professional studies alongside the traditional madrasa curriculum, unlike the tradition of teaching eighteenth-century Dars-e-Nizami inside madrasas. Islamic school students complete tenth grade at the same time as the public and private school students and move on to pursue degrees at colleges and universities. In this way, they enter the job market like other graduates, rather than like the madrasa graduates, who may remain unemployed outside the theological studies realm.

In the following table, I summarize the Islamic school curriculum to highlight why they are more attractive for well-to-do Muslim patrons than either madrasas or private secular schools.

Islamic schools are a significant educational phenomenon for having created a new image of Islamic education students. Instead of sitting on cold floors memorizing the Quran, Islamic school students understand the Arabic grammar of the Quran while sitting in modern school classrooms in bright uniforms. Confident schoolboys

Table 3.4 Subjects Taught in Islamic Schools and Their Nature of Inclusion

Subjects	Nature of Inclusion
English	Yes. Of PSS standard.
Hifz/Quranic memorization	Yes. Of M standard.
Nazira (Quranic reading)	Yes. Of M standard.
Urdu	Yes. Of PSS standard.
Physics, Biology, Chemistry	Yes. Of PSS standard.
Social Studies and Pakistan Studies	Yes. Of PSS standard.
O-levels	Yes. Of PSS standard.
National Matric (O-levels equivalent) system	Yes. Of PSS standard.

Abbreviations: PSS = Private Secular School; M = Madrasa

confidently hold their Islamic books and make eye contact. Montessori boys are shown in bright and colorful classrooms with stylish low benches neatly lined up against the walls, and disc-style board games in the center. These are deliberate attempts to distance Islamic education from dark, dingy rooms with plain walls where boys sit in front of table-length, immovable Qurans, expressionless, moving back and forth all day memorizing it.

In the next chapter, I will continue discussing how Islamic schools create multiple realities by de-essentializing the notion of "Islamic" in relation to the ideologies of the schools' entrepreneurs and patrons.

CHAPTER 4

Examining Diversity in Islamic Schools

In this chapter, I examine the varieties of Islamic schools in Karachi and the ways in which they cater to the sectarian, ethnic, communal, and political ideologies of various communities. Knowledge is conditioned by the situation of its producer. The production of knowledge and the validity of its contents are intimately connected with the social position of its producers.[1] The interests to which Islamic schools cater depend on the ideologies and educational outlook of the schools' diverse entrepreneurs. I examine how the backgrounds of Islamic school entrepreneurs change the meaning of Islamic education, how these affect pedagogies and the environment for Western-style, modern secular education in these schools, and how they create varied class, ethnic, religious, and national subjectivities.

Being the largest city, seaport, and financial center of Pakistan, Karachi is home to diverse religions, Islamic sectarian traditions, ethnicities, and linguistic and communal groups. The Karachi Islamic schools follow different Islamic traditions based on (*madhab*) of the school administration. For the purpose of my study, I will divide them into (1) the madrasa-alumni-operated (MA) Islamic schools and (2) the commercial (C) Islamic schools.

The first kind of Islamic schools are traditional, conservative, and closer in pedagogies to madrasas. They implement Islamic conduct and curriculum more rigorously and are sensitive to madhab traditions. These schools, generally opened next to the madrasa, are less expensive since tuition is subsidized by donations and endowments from the parent madrasa. To highlight how Islamic schools are divided along sectarian lines, my examples in this chapter will draw from two schools following the Deobandi variety of Sunni sectarian tradition, three examples from the Barelvi Sunni variety of Islamic schools, one from the Ahl al-Hadith Sunni variety, and two from the Shiite madrasa-alumni-operated ones.

The C Islamic schools in Karachi are not run by people formally trained in *fiqh*. They are operated by entrepreneurs from business families or from educated professionals who are running the school as a side business or a post-retirement enterprise. C Islamic schools are liberal and similar to the modern private secular schools in their outlook. Although not divided along sectarian lines, the C Islamic schools still cater to diverse social considerations. In my examination of this type, I provide one example of the commercial Sunni kind, one example of the commercial Shiite kind, one of the politico-religious kind opened by Jamaat-e-Islami, and one of an ethnic kind opened by the Memon linguistic business community. Lastly, I present a brief comparison of Islamic schools and the non-Muslim private parochial schooling in the city through the example of one such Zoroastrian school.

Moral Code of Conduct in Madrasa-Alumni-Operated (MA) and Commercial (C) Islamic Schools

In both MA and C Islamic schools that I visited, the lack of adequate classroom space encouraged coeducational classrooms at the primary level. However, at the secondary level, the classes are gender-segregated. In the MA Islamic schools, Islamic principles are more strictly enforced. Both students and female faculty have to follow strict purdah. All female staff must wear an *abaya*. The boys are required to wear *kameez shalwar*, Pakistan's national dress, a knee-length full-sleeve shirt with loose trousers. All male students and staff must wear prayer caps. This is in contrast to the private secular schools, where boys wear dress pants and short-sleeved shirts. The difference in the style of dress is to designate the Islamic school environment as Islamic by promoting the national dress as opposed to the colonial one (dress pants and shirts). In most of the C Islamic schools, however, boys wear dress pants and shirts. They wear prayer caps only at the time of Quranic recitation during morning assembly or at the afternoon prayer time. However, in the case of girls, Islamic mode of dress is not relaxed. Girls wear *kameez shalwar* and head scarves. In both kinds of Islamic schools, men are not allowed to wear half-sleeved shirts if they are in Western attire. Female students are required to wear scarves. Due to dress codes and gender segregation, particularly at the secondary level, girls and boys have separate sport periods. The sports grounds are usually in such a position with respect to the school buildings that boys or girls cannot look out at the field from the classroom during each other's sports hours.[2]

A Look at MA Islamic Schools

Read (a pseudonym), is one of the oldest experiments in MA Islamic schools. Read began as a chain of Quranic-memorization schools only, to which secular schools were later attached. I met with the chairperson, who explained Read to me:

> Three madrasa graduates, trained in Dars-e-Nizami [eighteenth-century syllabus followed in South Asian madrasas], got together and began a *Hifz* program. Public demand turned us into a school. We're the only school that began the tradition of daytime schooling in the country. Other private schools are too Westernized. Saint this, saint that, convent this, convent that . . . you tell me, what percentage of Pakistan identifies with that? But they all go there for education; however, the students come out averted from their religion and class-conscious. They do not come out as Muslims. In Islam, there is no class . . . It is a sin for a Muslim to choose between worldly and religious education.

I next asked the chairperson why a student must become a *hafiz* instead of a good Quranic reader. He seemed prepared for such questions and replied,

> I ask you, why didn't you buy a pamphlet off the street and say that you had a degree? Because you did not think that you would be master in a field until you aimed for more precise knowledge. We make students memorize the Quran so that they graduate as scholars of theology, at least at the junior level. We are not like other madrasas you may have visited. We conduct regular tests in Quranic comprehension before we consider a student good in Quranic memory.[3]

I was next given a tour of the Quranic memorization classrooms, where students sat on carpeted floors with their Qurans placed on low benches, the standard seating arrangement in madrasas. Through this practice, Read school administration recreates the visual and spatial environment of madrasas while offering employment promising secular education. Alima Ayesha (woman Islamic scholar), who gives tajvid lessons at the school, said, "We don't just say Islamic and then have a routine school experience. This school puts into practice the core values of piety and morality. We have separate buildings for girls and boys. Students are taught by same gender teachers."[4]

1. Madrasa-Alumni-Operated Islamic Schools: Sunni Subsectarian Pedagogical Differences

Due to their affiliation with madrasas that strictly adhere to one Sunni or Shiite subsect or the other, MA Islamic schools do not tolerate students and staff from other sects. The Sunni MA Islamic schools are further divided into at least three major subsects: the Deobandi, the Barelvi, and the Ahl al-Hadith. This is also the order of the dominance of these sects in the country.

1a) The Deobandi Islamic Schools

The Deoband school of thought, the inspiration for the Taliban, follows a puritanical Islam based on Quran and Sunna alone. The Deobandis disagree with the Barelvi practice of *naat* (singing praise of Prophet Muhammad), and their conceptualization of Prophet Muhammad and regard these practices as bida (later innovations to Islamic teachings). At a MA Islamic school affiliated with a madrasa offering the puritanical Deobandi Sunni form of Islamic education and located in Guru Mandir, a lower-middle- to middle-class area of Karachi, I asked the chairperson what sectarian tradition his school followed. He asked me what I meant. I asked him if Shiite tradition was also taught in the school. He replied firmly, "There is only one form of Islam. If any other sect wants to learn it, we are open to it, but our Islam is only Quran or Sunna." I asked about who enrolls in the school. He said, "Students from the Read network of madrasas join in the secondary stage. We are open to students from other madrasas, but we first test their Islamic knowledge and Quranic comprehension. We do a crash course for them to catch up with the secular education, but such students are usually placed at an advanced level in the Hifz class." I asked if graduates from other madrasas, such as the Sufism-oriented Barelvi madrasas enroll in his school. He said, "No, like I said, we do Quran and *sunna*. No innovational Islam." I asked him if any Deobandi could join. He said, "Yes. As long as they have received some form of religious schooling at home before."[5]

The chairperson's comments highlight the fact that Islamic tradition has a different meaning in each Islamic school. As I sat in on the tenth-grade Islamiat class at his school, I noticed that the class lecture was structured around reading and translation of Quranic verses with the exclusion of all debates on the prophet's form and divinity and other esoteric practices that are integral to the Barelvi Islamic tradition.[6] I heard the teacher, Maulvi Inayatullah, explain a saying of Prophet Muhammad that warned the Muslims of the wrath of God against those who strayed from following his word. As an example, Maulvi Inayatullah used the Mughal dynasty, the last glorious era of Muslim rule in India, after which the British occupied the region, as an example. "What led to the failure of the Mughals?" he asked, looking around at the students.

The innovations made to Allah's word by the kings. There was music, saint worship, and shrine-building going on while the British came and sacked the place. Today, no one associates glory with the Muslims. They associate the Twin Towers attacks with them. How can the Muslims redeem themselves? By uniting the *ummah* (Muslim polity) . . . by condemning extra-religious practices that are being practiced in our country in the name of religious tradition and returning to *real Islam*.[7]

As Maulvi Inayatullah emphasized, his school stands for the continuation of the puritanical, Sunni tradition that was first revived through the Deobandi Sunni madrasas in British India in the nineteenth century. The motivation then was to rid Muslim education and practice of all innovation in order to revive a discrete and monolithic Muslim identity that could stand against the injustices of the colonial rule.[8] In Maulvi Inayatullah's Islamic school, the engagement with modern secular education occurs through the revival of a "non-innovational," orthodox form of Sunni Islam that can reassert a nonscandalous Pakistani

Muslim identity. MA Islamic schools like Maulvi Inayatullah's seem to be critiquing the notion that Islamic education creates homogeneous religious subjectivities and highlights Asad's argument that Islamic tradition cannot be defined as a monolithic whole, but as the practice that responds to a particular historical condition in the past.[9]

In March 2008, on one of my visits to an MA Islamic school following the Deobandi Sunni subsect, I joined the staff and students for the afternoon prayers. The *imam*, teachers, and administrators began directing students to return to their classes in lines. Some students individually prayed after the prayers, but they were ignored. This manner of incorporating Islamic practice stood in contrast to the way in which I saw after-prayers collectively recognized in the Barelvi Islamic schools. The fact that an Islamic practice celebrated in a Barelvi school is not celebrated in a Deobandi school highlights the diverse ways in which Islamic tradition is defined and incorporated in modern secular education. In the fourth-grade Islamiat class that I sat in on the same day, Ms. Sajida, a graduate of a Deobandi madrasa, read the first two paragraphs of the lesson,

> Enemies of our Faith: As Muslims, our duty is to protect our faith from non-Muslim aggressors and from Muslim dissenters who commit the sin of sharing the power of Almighty Allah. May God forgive our sins and direct us towards His [Allah] and His beloved Prophet, Moḥammad Peace Be Upon Him's true teachings.[10]

During the recess, I asked a ninth grader, Tasneem, preparing for her preliminary exams in school to participate in the nationwide ninth- and tenth-grade combined exam, who, in her opinion, could the Muslim dissenters be. After much deliberation and consultation with her friends, she said, "I don't know . . . like people who go to the Sufi [saint] shrines and practice idolatry."[11]

In textbooks, class lectures, and prayer practices, the Deobandi Islamic schools stand in contrast to the Barelvi ones. Deobandi schools stay open during the anniversaries of the prophet's birth and death. The schools' doors are only open to Sunni Deobandis, or, as Ms. Sajida pointed out, "Staff and students who understand that there is no place for music, chanting and any mediation between man and Allah in Islam."[12]

1b) The Barelvi Islamic Schools

The Barelvis in Pakistan, representing the traditional dominant Islamic tradition of South Asia, were outnumbered in the 1980s, when, under Zia-ul-Haq's Islamization, Saudi money led to the establishment of many madrasas sympathetic to the Wahhabi school of thought of Saudi Arabia, called Deobandis. In February 2008, I visited the female branch of an MA Islamic school of the Barelvi kind. I sat in on a fifth-grade class on a Friday, the day for special afternoon prayers for Muslims. After English, math, and science, it was time for the Islamic education. The teacher opened the textbook in Urdu, printed by the Jamaat Ahle Sunnat, the religious organization representing Barelvis own publishing house. She read out the question to the class, "What is Prophet Muhammad's (peace be upon him, PBUH) personality?" Students raised their hands, and Rehana was chosen to answer. Four more students answered the question in more or less the same words. The teacher then read out the second question, "How can we communicate with Prophet Muhammad?" Another girl answered, "Our holy *pir* [religious mendicants], blessed by the grace of Allah, can help us communicate with Rasul Allah [Prophet of Allah]." The teacher asked, "Is prophet *bashar* [human material]?" She smiled and looked around the class, "This is a short answer. You all should know. All together." The students answered in chorus what seemed a memorized answer: "Prophet Muhammad Peace Be upon Him is not *bashar*. He is made out of *nur* [light]."[13]

Only in the Barelvi school of thought is Prophet Muhammad represented as immortal. The Barelvi MA Islamic schools are attended by students from non-Deobandi Sunni families. They represent the sectarian differences that differentiate the Islamic educational experiences of students at every Islamic school.

At 1:00 PM in the Barelvi school mentioned above, students from all grades were convened at the prayer hall. I joined the prayer ritual that was followed by after-prayers, a manner of incorporating Islamic practice that I only saw in these schools. Next, a completely veiled teacher came to the microphone and said the *durood* (phrases that venerate Prophet Muhammad) and then announced Naheed from grade 8 to come up for *naat*. Naheed's mature voice echoed at the microphone as she sang about Prophet Muhammad's welcome in Medina, a joyous occasion. As she concluded, the assembly, students, and staff, instantly exclaimed, "Jazak Allah!" (May Allah reward you!)[14] Such *naat* performances, considered by the Deobandis as a later invention and therefore un-Islamic, are held several times a year. *Naat* competitions are also held between Barelvi Islamic schools throughout the city. Hamd (hymns) competitions are also held. Sitting in a seventh-grade Islamiat (Islamic studies) class at another Barelvi Islamic school, I learned that the students are prepared and tested on the biographies of famous Sufi saints of South Asia and their practices. Besides Quran and Sunna, the teacher taught religious chanting and belief in intercession between humans and Divine Grace through an ascending, linked, and unbroken chain of holy personages, pir, reaching ultimately to Prophet Muhammad, who intercede on behalf of humans with Allah. Many Barelvi Islamic schools stay open on Prophet Muhammad's birth anniversary to celebrate it.[15]

Under British rule, the Deobandis began their madrasas as a puritanical movement to rid the Muslim community of the Sufi saint mediation that the Deobandis claimed was adopted while living with the non-Muslims. Those who accepted this intercession as Islamic, the Barelvis, rejuvenated their own Barelvi madrasas to make Muslims visible to the British as they negotiated political rights of the colonized in India. The Barelvi Islamic schools in Karachi continue this tradition in a unique way. At the third O-level Barelvi school I visited in a lower-middle-class neighborhood of Karachi, the secondary school students were celebrating the student activities day. The house system is a traditional feature of British schools and is still followed in the public and private secular schools of Pakistan. It refers to groups of pupils separated by grade levels and divided for intra- and inter-school activities. In the activities, the students represented four houses that were named after four Barelvi Sufi scholars of South Asia. An important part of it was the debate competition, a common student activity in Pakistani public and private secular schools. The competition was between eighth through tenth graders. The ninth-grade student representing the Ahmed Raza Khan Fazil-e-Barelvi House won. The school then formed an assembly. The chief guest was the leader of the Islamic movement Dawat-al-Islam—active in seventy-four countries—who owns a large area in Karachi for his *naat* and *dua*-reading congregations. The ninth grader was called up to the stage to receive his award, and the ninth-grade students standing parallel to the eighth and the tenth graders booed them and cheered for their house. "Fazil-e-Barelvi is a better saint!" "Saint Qadri [the tenth-grader's house] must be turning over in his grave right now!"[16]

This contrasted with the kinds of houses sometimes found in private secular schools, where houses are usually named after colors or regions of the country. The unique phenomenon in the Barelvi schools is that the students cheer for their own saints, and the houses construct scholars of their own subsect of Sunni Islam as the leaders to look up to. The way the ninth graders booed the eighth and tenth graders highlights how extracurricular and sport activities are tied to a particular Islamic tradition in Islamic schools; the house that wins does not win praise for the activity or the student, but only for the Saint.

1c) The Ahl al-Hadith Islamic Schools

Ahl al-Hadith Islamic schools follow the Ahl al-Hadith sectarian tradition. The term Ahl al-Hadith literally means "People of *hadith*." It is an Islamic reformist movement and school of thought. The adherents consider themselves free to seek guidance in matters of religious faith and practices from the authentic traditions, *hadith*, which together with the Quran are in their view the principal worthy guide for Muslims. In 1988, during the Saudi-inspired Islamization policy of Zia-ul-Haq, the number of Ahl al-Hadith madrasas in Pakistan was 134. More than any other kind of madrasa in the country, the Ahl al-Hadith madrasas had grown to 310 in number by the year 2000, showing a 131 percent increase.[17] The Ahl al-Hadith groups are described as "puritans," and sometimes Wahhabis, after the puritanical movement in Saudi Arabia, and the majority follows the lead of the ulema of Saudi Arabia.

Student from grades 7–10 prepare a *hadith* with translation and explanation every day and present it during the assembly. During my visit to an Ahl al-Hadith Islamic school, I observed that there was Quranic recitation in the assembly. When it ended, a senior student came up to the microphone with a piece of paper in hand. He first demonstrated that he knew the *hadith* in Arabic by heart, putting the paper in his pocket. He then folded his hands on his chest, closed his eyes in concentration, and recited the *hadith*. He then translated it in Urdu. Next, he took out the tafsiror explanation regarding the *hadith*. Students seek their *nazira* and *hifz* teacher, Ms. Hajra, to prepare for the assembly. I said to Ms. Hajra that it seemed that *hadith* is an important part of the school's Islamic education. She said, "Yes. We follow the Ahl al-Hadith interpretation." I asked if that brought her school closer to the madrasas. She answered plainly, "We are a school just like the other ones. We are not a madrasa, because we complete all curriculum requirements for private secular schools." I insisted that other Islamic schools do not emphasize the *hadith* the same way when they teach their Islamic curriculum.

Ms. Hajra smiled, "Yes. It is because the students are too young to understand what exegesis they should refer to for more complex arguments in religion. Therefore, we teach them the sources that we believe are the closest to the spirit of Islam. Yes, that brings a difference of *maslak* [used as a synonym for madhab] maybe."

"How are students prepared for the morning assembly I had seen?" I asked. The teacher replied,

> Depending on whether the student is from class 7 and 8 or is at an advanced level, from class 9 and 10, I ask them if they have a particular *hadith* in mind. Then I check it to make the difficulty level and content appropriate so that it is understandable even for students in lower grades. I instruct them in where to take the exegesis from. The student you saw today is already a *hafiz* [one who has memorized the Quran].[18]

As evident from the above example, Islamic education in some Islamic schools translates into students' enculturation in the Barelvi tradition. The same day, I sat in on the school's tenth-grade O-level add (additional) math class and saw the same student who had presented his research on a *hadith* that morning. It was February, a stressful time for the students as they sat four days before the preliminary exam at the school (i.e., mock exams that would prepare the students to take the O-level exams at the British Council, Karachi, in May). As he intently listened to his instructor explaining a theorem, I could not help contrasting him, in an Ahl al-Hadith Islamic school, with students I had observed a month before during a visit to an Ahl al-Hadith madrasa, who memorized the Quran while listlessly moving back and forth in rhythm.[19]

1d) Shiite Madrasa-Alumni-Operated (SMA) Islamic Schools

The Shiite community in Karachi can be divided into two sects: Twelvers or Ithna Ashari, the majority Shiite sect in Pakistan, and Seveners or Ismailis. Both Ithna-Asheri and Ismailis believe in the same early imams, except that the former believe in Musa al-Khadim as the successor to the sixth *imam*, Imam Jafar al-Sadiq, and Ismailis believe in Ismail ibn Jafar as the successor to him. The Shiite Islamic schools are divided into those operated by the alumni of madrasas following either of these sects.

In the SMA Islamic schools in general, Islamic studies include knowledge about Muhammad's cousin Ali's succession to the caliphate, the elimination of Ali's family in the Battle of Karbala, and about the Shiite imams. For example, in the Islamiat class at one of the Sunni Islamic schools I visited, students recited the *kalima* (six compilations of Quranic verses that Muslims memorize), the profession of faith by a Muslim in the words, "There's no God but Allah, and Muhammad is his last prophet." Sitting in on grades 2 and 3 at two SMA Islamic schools located in the upper-class area of Defense and in the middle-class area of Rizvia Society, respectively, I found that the students recited, "Allah is one, Prophet Muhammad, his daughter Fatima, Imam Ali, and his sons the infinite five, *imams* are twelve, Prophet Muhammad, Fatima and the twelve *imams* are the innocent fourteen, and total prophets are one hundred and twenty-four thousand."[20]

The school observes Yom-e-Husayn, which commemorates the anniversary of the death of Imam Husayn, the grandson of Prophet Muhammad, with great zeal. Imam Husayn's anniversary is a regular day at a Sunni school. *Muharram*, the first month in the Islamic calendar and the most important month in Shiite history, marks the anniversary of the Battle of Karbala, when Imam Husayn ibn Ali, a grandson of Muhammad, the founder of Islam, and the third Shiite *imam* was killed by the forces of the second Umayyad caliph Yazid I. I visited three SMA Islamic schools in which *majalis* (congregations) are arranged in the Islamic month of *Muharram* in which Husayn was killed. In the Islamiat class in these schools, the syllabus is supplemented by special sessions in which the teachers inform students about the importance of *Muharram*. *Marsiya* (elegiac poem written to commemorate the martyrdom and valor of Hazrat Imam Husayn and his comrades at the

Battle of Karbala) are arranged several times a year in these schools, often coinciding with the birthdays of the Twelve *Imams*, in which both students and teachers participate. On *Ashura*, the tenth day of Muharram when the forces of Yazid are believed to have killed Husayn his family, and around seventy-two supporters in the Battle of Karbala, the SMA as well as the commercial Shiite Islamic schools are closed.[21]

i.) Shiite Islamic Schools: The Saturday School Variety
Saturday school is a third, unique kind of Shiite Islamic school. As the name indicates, it is held on Saturdays only. Saturday school is separate for boys and girls. There are two branches of the school, one in PECHS, an upper-middle-class area, and another in Defense, an upper-class area of Karachi. However, in the Defense campus, it is held three times a week. A teacher said to me jokingly, "It's necessary to have it three times a week in Defense than anywhere else in Karachi. Those people are so *out* [of control and manners] and Westernized nobody needs more religious counseling than them!"[22] As highlighted by the teacher's comment, elites living in Defense are associated with the kind of modernity that is equated with Westernization, perceived as a sign of demoralization of the society. The school's patrons conceive of Islamic schools as a means of apprising the culturally and morally estranged elite of their religious traditions.

I asked the Principal, Ms. Zainab, about the pedagogical ideology at the Saturday school in Defense. She said,

> This is an Islamic school. Boys and girls wear white. Girls wear shalwar *kameez* and boys pant shirts. It is compulsory for girls to wear scarves and boys to wear caps. But don't think that it is a madrasa. It emphasizes learning through play, and clears concepts such as Allah's oneness through games rather than rote learning. We have indoor and outdoor games regularly. Islamic education in the school is given using English textbooks that come from Iran. Since the school believes in teaching religion through games, the teachers are given a week's deadline to prepare games and activities for children.

I asked if non-Defense dwellers could afford the education. She said,

> It is for Sayyid Shiites, though Khoja Shiite children can also get admission. Besides, we keep the tuition cost low here, around Rs. 1000 [US$10]

per month, including stationary. The children get books free of cost that they return at the end of the year. It also offers scholarships that exempt 50 percent of the fee.[23]

Ms. Zainab's narrative is coded with the imagery of Islamic education as it has always been taught in madrasas. She was among several Islamic school patrons I interviewed who highlighted their seminary-style Islamic education as different from the seminaries because of the cognitive activities and games that erase the subservience and brainwashing madrasa students are subject to. As Ms. Zainab's narrative highlights, as much as Islamic schooling is about equating the prestigious O-level education with seminary-style Islamic education, the class inequality is sometimes recreated in ways that gentrify Islamic education. Ms. Zainab equates class with the elite, Defense-dwelling Shiite community around her school, which she assumes is Sayyid (people who claim to be descendants of Prophet Muhammad). Khojas are a distinct ethnolinguistic Shiite group. Not only is Sayyid a prestige marker by way of spiritual status for Ms. Zainab, but it also equates to a superior ethnicity, the Urdu-speaking majority Shiites rather than the minority, less educated, largely low-income Khoja Shiites. Following Bourdieu's understanding of capital, the built environment of Defense and the Sayyid prestige serves as the symbolic capital of Ms. Zainab's school.[24] They render the Islamic school an attractive educational choice for the elite Shiites. At the same time, Islamic tradition in this school is a means of making the minority Shiite minority visible. Therefore, some economic incentives are offered to include a few Shiite students from Khoja families who aspire for status elevation by association with a prestigious Islamic school in Defense and by socializing with students from elite Sayyid families.

The student-teacher ratio in public schools and madrasas is usually 1:50. Like other Islamic schools, Shiite Saturday schools attract upper-middle-class and upper-class families because of a higher teacher-student ratio. An O-level biology teacher at the Saturday school, Ms. Erum Zaidi contrasted this trend with private secular schools.

> The problem with those schools is that as soon as they become popular because of their quality of education, they get greedy and started filling in classes. One teacher for forty students. One might as well go to a public school! I have taught at private [secular] schools before. I

like teaching here because there are two teachers for a class of twenty students all the way to eighth grade [last pre-O-level grade]. And they don't become business-minded and not care about piety. Even if we get ten students per class, each class has two sections, one for boys and one for girls.[25]

Ms. Zaidi is one of the many female staff who covers their heads following the school's dress code for female staff and students. Later that day, I was given a spot at a distance to watch the secondary boys sections come out with a male PT (physical training) teacher for workout routines, racing, and soccer, which is the typical boy school sport in the country. The girl sections continued with other periods on the third floor of the building. Two hours later, the girls came down with their own female PT teacher, and, after workouts, played handball, the typical girls sport in the country. The school followed a kind of gender segregation not followed in private secular schools. All boys sections were on the second floor, from where they could not look up at the girls.[26]

The Shiite Saturday Islamic school, as highlighted by Ms. Zainab and Ms. Erum Zaidi's perspectives, is a unique blend of schooling. Through a socially elite, Defense environment, predominantly Sayyid clientele, amenities of private schooling such as a sports and student-teacher ratio, manner of imparting Islamic education and piety in an O-level system unlike madrasas, and a distinctly Shiite communal atmosphere, the school is able to create various sectarian, religious, class-economic, religious and symbolic, ethnic, and modern subjectivities in the students.

The Shiite Saturday school is open from 10:00 AM–12:30 PM and takes children from four to fourteen years. I saw all the students pray in the congregation following Shiite rituals. The school gives moral/religious education through games, for example, one was called "cash for good deeds." The school keeps its own currency called "*sawaab* (reward for good deeds) bills." They are awarded as cash prizes to students who pray five times a day and perform other obligations of a good Muslim. A fair is then held at the end of the year in which the students who accumulate the most *sawaab* bills can buy whatever they like.[27] "And they display really nice and expensive things; it's for real," stressed a fourth grader's parent while talking to me.[28]

2. Commercial Islamic Schools

2a) *The Sunni Variety*

Commercial (C) Islamic schools are closer in pedagogies to private secular schools and treat Islamic education like other secular subjects. Jamil and his wife, Hafsa for example, a couple in their thirties who live in a one-bedroom apartment in a lower-income area of Lyari Town in Karachi, have chosen to send their son, Ehtesham, to a commercial Islamic school close to their house. I asked, "Do you aspire that Ehtesham become a Hafiz-e-Quran?"

"No, the school does not have *hifz* and that kind of detailed Islamic instruction," said Jamil. "We do not see him become an alim," he chuckled, watching while Ehtesham, a fourth grader, bit into a Wall's Cornetto, the European ice cream that had recently bought off the local Polka and became a class symbol. "He must know how to pray, how to read Quran correctly, and other schools don't have *tajvid,* and they make *namaz* part of your daily routine. So it is hard for us to reinforce it separately." Hafsa added, "They have a PT [physical training] period . . . he likes to run."[29] I visited Ehtesham's school and observed that, compared to the MA Islamic schools, gender segregation at the secondary level was not strict. Boys and girls sit in the same room but at two ends of the class, or there is one row of boys-only and another of girls-only. While the school building was smaller than other Islamic schools in Karachi, it was similar to the commercial Islamic schools I visited that were not opened by madrasa graduates. Not only did those commercial Islamic schools have more relaxed gender boundaries in class and during recess time, but they also either did not have a Quranic memorization program, or one that was optional or elective. The Islamic education does not favor any sectarian tradition, and administrators, staff, teachers, and students from any Sunni subsect may join the schools. However, it is less common for Shiites to join a Sunni school. Out of the four commercial Sunni Islamic schools I visited, I found Shiite students in only two, four in the first case and one in the second case. In none of the schools were the administration and teachers Shiites.[30]

2b) *The Shiite Variety*

In Pakistan, there exist private secular schools that are run by Shiites. In the nationwide matriculation examination, two Islamiat papers are made: one for Sunni students and one for the Twelver Shiite students. The exam does not necessarily reflect their choice of schooling, and it is common to see Sunnis studying in Shiite private secular schools and vice versa. The Shiite-established schools present Shiite theology differently from the Sunni schools.

Liberal Shiite private schools accept both Shiite and Sunni students. In grades 9 and 10, the Shiite students appear in the Shiite Islamiat nationwide public exam, and Sunni children appear in the Sunni Islamiat exam. However, as a Shiite private secular school student told me, "Many students find that learning about the history and institution of Imamate in addition to the regular/Sunni Islam course is too hard. So, at the time of the annual Islamic studies exam, they declare themselves as Sunni and take the easier exam!"[31]

The Shiite Islamic schools that are more commercial in nature and/or follow a less rigorous religious curriculum only teach *nazira* classes and are relaxed in their gender and spatial rules. I spoke to a senior teacher of math at a Shiite school about their exam ideology. She rolled her eyes and said,

> I know that old trick . . . of Shiite kids taking Sunni Islamiat exams because it is shorter and easy . . . That is why we had to establish a Shiite Islamic school, because even though there are other private schools opened by the Shiite community, the administration does not obligate Shiite students to understand their own *aqaid* [theology]. Children then move on to secular colleges and universities in a predominantly Sunni environment without ever knowing that they belong to a Shiite family!"[32]

The Shiite Islamic studies that the math teacher mentioned in her school includes poems commemorating the *imams* at the primary level and the history and contributions to jurisprudence and the society of the Pious Caliphs and the *imams*. In addition, the episodes of Ali's succession and of the Battle of Karbala are studied in detail, and the founders of the Ummayad Dynasty are described as the enemies of Islam in the textbooks. Contrastingly, the Sunni Islamic schools teach about the Pious Caliphate after Prophet Muhammad, and how it was succeeded by the Umayyads and the

Abbasids. Shiite Islamic schools also celebrate the birthdays of all the Twelve Imams.[33]

ii.) Shiite Islamic Schools: A Note on the Minority Ethnic Varieties
A small percentage of the Shiite community in Karachi is also represented by the Ismailis, among whom Khojas are a prominent ethnic community. Some Shiite Islamic schools in Karachi are also patronized by the Khojas. Over the years, Khojas spread to different parts of the world. In Pakistan, Khojas are concentrated in Sindh, and especially in Karachi. The community is comprised of Hanafi Sunnis, but it is predominantly Shiite. The Khoja Ithna Ashari Shiite Islamic schools largely cater to the Khoja community, although the school is open to non-Khoja Shiites, but not to Sunni Muslims.

As for the Ismaili community at large, schools similar to the Islamic schooling trend have been opened by the Nizarisect, under the Aga Khan Development Network headed by the Aga Khan IV, current *imam* of the Nizari Ismaili Muslims. Another large community representing the Ismailis in Pakistan, the Dawoodi Bohras can be regarded as the earliest people who established their own Islamic schools in 1983. However, similar to the Aga Khani/Ismaili, Islamic schools are ways for Dawoodi Bohras to represent their identity as a religious, linguistic, and ethnic minority rather than in response to the radicalization of the Pakistani madrasas and their association with religious extremism. Like the Memon schools, teachers, students, and administrators in the Khoja Shiite, Aga Khani, and Dawoodi Bohra Islamic schools frequently communicate in their communal languages rather than in Arabic. Thus, the schools do not simply offer one kind of Islamic education. Instead, their pedagogies are tailored to perpetuate the sectarian interests of their owners, teachers, and patron families. However, it is sometimes not the sectarian interests of the citizens but ethnic and communal interests that guide the curricula.

Based on difference in the backgrounds of the school entrepreneurs, the learning environment and interpretation of Islamic tradition may be different. In addition to the differences in religious outlook, Islamic schools show diversity based on two more differences in the producers: politico-religious and ethnic. In the section below, I will highlight how these differences influence Islamic school pedagogies.

3. The Politico-Religious Islamic Schools

Some Islamic schools have also been established by religious political parties. For example, the Jamaat-e-Islami (JI), a Sunni Deobandi religious political party, has opened up its own network of Islamic schools. JI was founded by Sayyid Abul Ala Maududi on August 26, 1941, in Lahore and is the oldest religious political party in Pakistan.

Since JI also has a separate network of madrasas in the country, their madrasa alumni head their Islamic schools. Usually families who are active members of, or vote for JI, send their children to these schools. However, other Sunni families, due to proximity of the school, also send children to the JI schools.

JI base support lies in the salaried middle classes. I visited a JIMA Islamic school in the middle-income area of Gulistan-e-Jauhar. The school had separate campuses for girls and boys. Similar to other Islamic schools, faculty for mathematics, general science, and other secular subjects were hired on merit basis at both primary and secondary levels. However, as the administration informed me, "Their strong adherence to Islamic practice was preferred."[34] Veiling was strictly enforced for the female staff, students, and faculty. JI's dawa network in financial, administrative, and academic networks is so vast that usually JI supporters or Muslims sympathetic to JI's version of Islam join as teachers.[35]

I sat in on the grade 6 social studies class in the JIMA Islamic schools. The teacher lectured on a chapter about our duties as citizens in a textbook published by JI's own publishing house. The students were to answer questions based on the reading passage. The first question was: "What are our duties as Muslims?" The students raised their hands to answer. The student chosen answered, "To save our culture from non-Muslims values that are not according to the path shown to us by Allah." The teacher elaborated on what those values could be—not being dutiful toward one's parents and cultivating the values of individualism and materialism.[36] Due to the British colonial memory, in popular discourse in Pakistan, Western culture is equated with imperialism. Hence, values such as collectivism and sharing are regarded as particular to Pakistani culture. In the case of this social studies lesson, the bad values of materialism and individualism are regarded not only as antidotes to Pakistani and Muslim values, but also as the defining feature of the non-Muslim world.

The lesson continued to discuss Pakistan's geography. The focus was on highlighting how its geographical location and resources were significant for the Islamic world. Such changes in the social and Pakistan studies syllabi that plotted Pakistan in a wider Islamic *ummah* geography rather than in world geography had first been introduced under Zia's Islamization. The JIMA Islamic school continues to follow that discourse in the social and Pakistan studies syllabi, as it accords with its own politico-religious ambition to bring Islamic rule in Pakistan. The teacher asked the next question on the lesson: "What is our role as citizens of Pakistan?" Another student raised her hand and answered, "To help Muslims not only in our country, but also internationally." The teacher elaborated on the answer by using Palestine as an example and pointed out that it is our duty as Pakistanis and as Muslims to help our brothers attain their freedom.[37]

Middle-class JI educational activists, teachers, and parents aspire to promote a blend of education that strengthens the professional credentials of the white-collar class through the O-level style of modern secular education and that strengthens the ideology of the party. In the JIMA Islamic schools, the kinds of national subjectivities created through the pedagogical process are considered an integral part of the students' religious subjectivities. Becoming a better citizen of the *ummah* is equated with becoming a good Pakistani. The teacher's elaboration on what helping other Muslims means forwards Jamaat-e-Islami's political agenda of molding the interests of the Pakistani state toward global Muslim struggles. In the JIMA schools, students' sense of civic duty and citizenship is geared toward making Islamic law central to state laws and policies.

4. The Linguistic/Communal Islamic Schools

As Karachi is home to people from diverse religious, national, sectarian, ethnic, and communal backgrounds, some Islamic schools are operated by and cater to Sunni Memons, the largest business community in Karachi. Memons are a predominantly mercantile community and are generally referred to as the "business community" in the country. A largely Sunni Muslim Sunni group, the Karachi Memons predominantly adhere to the Hanafi Sunni sub-sect, which is dominant in the country, and have opened Islamic schools for their community in their residential enclaves in the city.

The Memons have a unique system of *jamaats* or *jamaat khanas* (congregations) for the welfare of the community and for preserving social relationships between Jamaat members. Being part of this global village, the community has also crossed national boundaries, and today a large number from the community live in the United States, United Kingdom, and so forth. The diaspora *jamaat khanas* send their remittances to those in Pakistan to support welfare projects, notably, the Memon schooling projects. Until now, the Memon schools were private secular and in those areas of Karachi where the community was large. With the emergence of the Islamic schooling trend, ex-patriots from Arab Gulf countries and countries in the West have begun pouring in remittances to establish and maintain these schools throughout Karachi. These Memon Islamic schools transmit the Sunni Islamic tradition and are open to all Sunnis, but only a nominal percentage of non-Memon Sunnis actually enroll in these schools.

In Karachi, the Memons of Kutch speak Kutchi, which is a hybrid of Sindhi, the provincial language. Similar to other Islamic schools, English is the medium of instruction, and Urdu is among other secular subjects. However, the use of Kutchi by teachers, staff, students, and administration in and outside the classrooms is common in the Kutchi Memon Islamic schools. Unlike the Islamic schools that stress the use of Arabic to signify Islamic knowledge, in the communitarian Memon Islamic school, teachers, administrators and students frequently switch to the Memoni dialect.

In Memon Colony, a lower-middle-class area of Karachi, I got an appointment for a formal interview with the founder and principal of a Memon Islamic school, Abdullah Memon, who told me about himself and his school. He introduced himself as a Sunni Memon, then saw me look to the wall of 3-D posters of upcoming apartment complex construction projects and explained:

> I am involved in the construction business. I have developed a curriculum for regular, secular schooling that simultaneously lays emphasis on Islamic values. I thought of starting this textbook project to do some good for my community. I just want to introduce an Islamic-oriented curriculum in it because nowadays even doctors don't know how to pray. People become so highly educated and don't even know the basics

of Islam. This curriculum is simply designed to give simple knowledge of Islam.

I asked what *maslak* the curriculum would be based on.

Just normal [read Sunni Islam]. We can't do away with differences based on *maslak,* but this course is not designed to point out such differences. Any student in any school can follow it. Whenever there will be a need to acknowledge different *maslaks,* we will acknowledge that certain schools of thought interpreted Islam differently. The purpose is to apprise people about the basics of Islam.

Next, the principal stressed the economic feasibility of his school: "Fee in my school is only Rs. 250 [US$2.50]. Can you tell me of any other school where it is such? These days, people cannot afford to send their children to school because of the fees. Tell me the least fees in the smallest private school?" I guessed it to be at least Rs. 1,000 (US$10) a month. He looked at me critically. "Good enough. Now tell me, even if a person has only two kids, how can he pay that fee, plus the expenditure on books, plus the uniforms, and so on and so forth?" He continued,

> This school is my experiment with this new kind of curriculum. Once the textbooks click, I will introduce them in a network of schools. I have already spoken to other businessmen and philanthropists in the Memon community to invest in the land, resources, and staff for this network of schools. Network is not a problem for me; I have a very vast social network to make this dream possible.

I asked if his school would cater to the Memon community only or if children from other backgrounds also enroll. He replied plainly, "No, it will be for anyone and everyone. It will run like any other school."[38]

Even though Abdullah's Islamic school is open to all Karachiites regardless of their backgrounds, rarely do non-Memon parents send their children to a Memon Islamic school, as they find the linguistic, religious, and social environment in these schools very different from their own regional and ethnic traditions. Thus, in Islamic schools like Mr. Abdullah's, Islamic and O-level education using English and

Kutchi as the medium of education serves as an instrument for the upward mobility of poor Memons and as a means by which Memons can find increased representation of their community in the white-collar job market of Karachi.

Creating Gender and Class Subjectivities

At another Memon Islamic school in Memon Colony, a predominantly Memon area of Karachi, my informant, a ninth grader named Zaibunnisa, helped me understand how gender subjectivities are constructed and transformed by the Memon citizens of Karachi through Islamic schooling. The school was unique in that it was closely tied to the vocational training courses for the Memon community. The school, following the community norm, was gender-segregated at the secondary level. Sixth- to tenth-grade girls attended regular periods in math, science, Urdu, *nazira*, and *hifz* inside the building until 2:00 PM. Then they came out into the playground while some female teachers began making their way to classrooms to set them up for handicraft and vocational training courses. The guard, often the only male and sitting far away by the playground gate, allowed the girls to find shady spots under the trees, where they loosened their *abaya*. Then they collected money and sent the guard to the nearest store with snack orders. Zaibunnisa, after shouting at the guard for not walking quickly enough with the Coke bottle that six girls looked forward to sharing, told me how she felt about her Islamic school. "I like this school because whatever Maulvi sahib [polite way of addressing] teaches here is not *out of course*. The school is affiliated with the Sindh provincial board. I'll finish my O-level very soon, inshallah."[39]

Zaibunnisa's choice of Islamic school is based on her understanding that seminary-style Islamic education acquired through private tuitions at home from madrasa teachers amounts to illiteracy in the job market. Acquiring Islamic education through a modern, secular private school gives her the confidence that Islamic education is recognized at the school and valued as much as the other subjects, unlike the case in private secular schools.

I next asked her if she would study after finishing her O-level. She said, "Actually, I want to start taking wedding reception orders very soon. If I get married after getting the O-level result, it's okay . . . I can always supplement my husband's income. If not, then until I get married, I'll use the catering money for intermediate [high school] studies." Zaibunnisa ate the lunch she brought from home as she waited to get into her class. "I know cooking. I cook every day. I am taking this class because they show you how to make flowers, decorate dishes, and teach several non-continental dishes: Italian, Chinese, Mexican. So, I'm learning how it's done in big hotels [hotel restaurants] to get large orders . . . and to get ideas to do catering for parties with themes." Familiar with the Karachi Memon tradition of marrying within the family, I asked if she would marry a cousin. "Yes, but nothing has been arranged yet," she replied, then added,

> It's not about a suitor. But the suitor should be aware about the world around him, understand the Quran . . . be able to talk in English. Not just sit at his father's jewelry store. I am educated and I know English. My parents are pro-education and they know that a primary school pass will not be a suitable mate just because he is family.[40]

The bell rang to announce that the afternoon classes in home economics and vocational training had started. Zaibunnisa and other secondary school girls gathered their bags and notebooks, put their scarves back on their heads, and strolled into their separate typing, shorthand, stitching, cooking, and other classes.

In a gender-segregated community, girls like Zaibunnisa are using Islamic schools as a means to increase their role in the public sphere by finding opportunities for growth in an Islamic educational environment. For her, knowing English is a way to transform from the member of an isolated business community and become a professional in ways that identify her with the non-Memon urban middle and upper class. The English-medium Islamic school is her conduit to achieve this goal. As the fifteen-cent coke bottle came in and the girls shared it in greater than 85°F heat, I could not help but compare the difference in status between the students of this Islamic school with the students in commercial Islamic schools in the upper-class Defense area. Compared to the American-style meals I saw being ordered during break time that were a status marker in the Defense area Islamic schools, Zaibunnisa's school had come a long way in getting a community tuition rate to afford Islamic education, and through it an opportunity to acquire social and economic capital for upward class mobility.[41]

As one of the few girls in her community who had found the opportunity to complete the prestigious O-level education, the traditional picture of a suitor has also changed. She desired to marry someone who held similar social capital for class elevation through English-medium, O-level-style education and cognitive knowledge of the Quran, as opposed to simply reading and memorizing the script. In addition, studying at a Memon Islamic school gave Zaibunnisa the opportunities to develop a small-scale independent business in an Islamic environment and the ability to navigate among upper-class, educated families by catering for their theme-based dinners.

A Note on Non-Muslim Religious Schools

Parsis are members of the Zoroastrian community. Karachi has one of the largest populations of Parsis in Pakistan. Parsis have their own parochial schools in Karachi, some of which are in buildings that were important community centers before 1947. These are the only forms of Parsi religious schools that have operated since the establishment of Pakistan. Therefore, the Parsi schools are not similar to the Islamic schools that have emerged in the last decade or so. Parsi schools operate more like private secular schools because they are open to students from other religious backgrounds and to the celebration of other religious holidays as well. They are similar to the liberal Shiite Islamic schools in that they observe Parsi practices and important occasions but do not obligate students to learn Zoroastrianism.

The majority of the Parsi community is from the affluent class. Thus, in the case of the Parsi private schools, the location of the school does not connote the social class of its patrons. In a Parsi school, I observed teachers selecting students at both primary and secondary levels for rehearsals that made them miss their classes in preparation for the Nauroz celebration, the holiday on March 21 that celebrates the Zoroastrian and also the Iranian lunar new year. On March 21, there are no classes. The Parsi private school celebrated Muslim Eid festivals, Christmas, and the Holi festival of the Hindus in a similar fashion, though the all-day celebration is done for the

Muslim festivals only, since the majority of the students in the school are Muslims.

As a minority religion school, Parsi schools does not aim to redefine Muslim practice and education but to celebrate Pakistan's diversity in a secular manner and experience a sense of community with other Zoroastrian minorities of Karachi. Unlike the Memon Muslims of Karachi, Parsis were a favored minority under British rule and were among the first to learn British culture and education and work for the empire. Therefore, in the post-colonial educational environment, the Parsi schools, similar to the Christian convents, are prestigious because of their strict enforcement of English and an educated, elite culture. Therefore, a large number of Muslims go to these schools seeking upward class mobility.

Similar to the Barelvi Islamic schools, during a visit to a Zoroastrian private school, I observed an inter-school competition in which four houses of the school competed with other private secular schools. The houses competed in oratory competitions, typical in public and private schools in the country, singing competition, art competition, and in sports. The four houses that the students represented through their badges, house color, and sashes highlighted the ideology of the school. The first house was named after the school's Parsi founder; the second after the country's founder, Quaid-e-Azam; the third after Reza Shah Pahlavi, founder of the Pahlavi dynasty that ruled Iran before the 1979 revolution; and the fourth after Sir Lancelot Graham, the first British governor of Sindh. In this way, the first house symbolized the Zoroastrian minority of Pakistan, the second Quaid-e-Azam house represented the school's patriotic spirit as well as allegiance to the leader, who was married to a Zoroastrian, the third Pahlavi house represented the Iranian origin of the Zoroastrians and the pre-1979 revolution commitment to modernization that the Pahlavi ruler had and that the Karachi Zoroastrians supported in Iran, and the fourth house represented the British governor, who appreciated the local politicians of Karachi's province, Sindh, for their service to the country.[42] Where the Barelvi school activities are run in the names of saints of a subsect of Sunni Islamic tradition, the houses at the Zoroastrian private schools celebrate the plurality of Pakistan with the Zoroastrian minority community at its core.

Conclusion

Even though madrasas are also divided along sectarian, political, and sometimes ethno-sectarian lines, they do not share the commitment of the Islamic schools of providing a single, government-approved package of modern, secular education alongside Islamic education. In the private secular schools, the Islamiat curriculum does not respond to the various ideological needs of the students and the school administration. Islamic schools, allowing for the construction of multiple dispositions toward Islamic tradition, political goals, and ethnic identities, are therefore unique in comparison to madrasas and private secular schools.[43] The perceptions of Islamic school female teachers in turn have developed in response to the objective conditions of working in general and working at a private school in particular. Through private Islamic education, parents, administrators, and teachers seem to be making an effort to create an image of Islamic learning in Pakistan that is as promising and distinguished as modern, private secular schooling. In chapter 5, I discuss the aspirations and pedagogical activities that realize this mission.

CHAPTER 5

Knowledge at Play

During my fieldwork, I saw a variety of Islamic schools pedagogies, primarily because entrepreneurs from various backgrounds operated these schools, which changed the ideological drive. In this chapter, I will discuss how the aspirations of the producers and patrons of knowledge at these schools inform its pedagogies and the kinds of religious, class, and national subjectivities formed in the students. In understanding these subjectivities, one must not forget the role that the socially prestigious language, English, the religious prestigious language, Arabic, and the cultural and national language, Urdu, play.

To provide a framework for understanding the daily routine and experiences of people in Islamic schools, I will primarily draw from my ethnographic data from four Islamic schools that represent the greatest variety in terms of their establishment and pedagogy and include both primary (grades 1–5) and secondary (grades 6–10) education. As described in chapter 3, madrasas operate through three subsectarian educational boards of the Sunni sect and one sectarian board of the Shiite sect. Among the Sunni madrasas, some have been established by the religious political party Jamaat-e-Islami. The first of the four schools that I will use as an example is operated by Jamaat-e-Islami. As the party's base support comes from salaried middle-class Karachiites, the JIMA school is located in Gulistan-e-Jauhar, a middle-class neighborhood of the city. I will use abbreviated names for the schools to maintain privacy of the people associated with the schools. Therefore, the first school is referred to as JIMA (Jamaat-e-Islami madrasa-alumni-operated) Islamic school. The second Islamic school is from the same category, except that it is operated by Shiite madrasa alumni. I mention it as SMA (Shiite madrasa-alumni-operated) Islamic school. The third and fourth schools are examples of commercial (C) Islamic schools. I refer to them as C1 and C2 Islamic schools. I chose C1 because of its location in the middle- to lower-middle-class town of Gulshan-e-Iqbal. I chose C2 because it was in the Malir Cantonment area, primarily occupied by military and naval elites of the city. To provide the broader ideological pictures and perspectives of administrators, teachers, students, and parents at various Islamic schools, I will include some interviews and observations from other Islamic schools as well.

1. Islamic School Pedagogies: Creating Islamic Subjectivities

1a) Creating Islamic Subjectivities: Pre-primary Educational Program at Islamic Schools

Many Islamic schools follow the Montessori system of pre-primary education. The pre-primary education system that Pakistan inherited from the British was the kindergarten system. During the 1980s, as private secular schools grew, the Montessori trend was introduced, and today it runs parallel with the kindergarten system in these schools. The majority of Islamic schools follow the Montessori system. Some Islamic schools also offer the kindergarten system, while others offer nursery (also as old as kindergarten in Pakistan) and playgroup forms of pre-primary education. Islamic schools distinguish their Islamic education from that given in the madrasas by claiming that, whereas in madrasas, rote learning decreases a child's ability for analytical thinking, the Montessori system ensures original thinking and creativity in children before formal schooling starts. Now, due to Islamic schools competing with private secular schools with Islamic and Montessori training, the social prestige attached to the kindergarten system has diminished and the Montessori system has become the most attractive feature of pre-primary Western secular education for Karachiites.

At C1, I sat in on the Montessori class, squashed between two- to four-year-old kids as we all faced two Montessori directresses, Ms. Hina and Ms. Mehreen. The children gave me pleasing smiles, thinking that I might be a new, third teacher. "*Assalaamualeikum* [Peace to you all], children!" said Ms. Hina.

The children chorused back. "*Waaleikumus salaam* [and peace to you too]."

Ms. Hina then spoke in English. "Let's start today's work. Ms. Mehreen will tell you what we are going to do today."

Ms. Mehreen followed, "We will do numbers!" The children made varied quizzical faces. She asked, "Before we start . . . c'mon, tell us what you say before you start work." Some children stared blankly, while others guessed and hissed a B sound. The teacher hinted, "Bis . . ." The children picked up. "*Bismillah . . . hir-rehman . . . nir-rahim* [In the name of Allah, the Most Beneficent, the Most Merciful]." The teachers then distributed cards with the English number one. Children were supposed to write the number. Fifteen minutes later, the teachers distributed the number one in Urdu, and the children spent time copying it. Next, the teachers distributed the number in Arabic. The teachers then told the children to come one by one and place their numbers in three slots that they had labeled Urdu, English, and Arabic. The activity lasted an hour. After the children settled down, the teachers distributed a simple image of a globe. The children were asked to color different parts (continents) with crayons and to use blue where waves showed water. When all children finished the activity, Ms. Mehreen pointed at the globe and asked, "What is this?" She answered herself, "Earth! What is Earth? *Dunya* [Urdu for *Earth*]," she explained. The children then repeated the word for several minutes.

Ms. Mehreen taught them about the shape of the Earth, and that it is round. Ms. Hina then took over. "Who made the Earth?" she asked. "Who knows? Who will tell me?" Ms. Hina then gently explained, "Allah made the Earth." The children repeated the question and answer with the teacher for a few minutes. "Where is Allah?" Ms. Hina asked. Some kids shrugged. Others leaned in, listening. "Up there." She pointed toward the sky. The children looked up. "Can you see Allah?" The class replied in the negative. The Montessori ran until noon, and I left early to talk to the principal, amazed at the patience of teachers in their early twenties with the three- to five-year-olds.[1]

Through activities similar to those described above, teachers at C1 develop both cognitive and moral needs of the children from the pre-primary stage. This is in sharp contrast to the environment at a typical madrasa (see chapter 3). Two teachers are in charge of a Montessori class, where the class number usually does not exceed thirteen. In this way, unlike the big classes at public schools and madrasas, individual attention is given to each student to build a framework of reasoning in them in which both worldly knowledge and religious beliefs are open to critical thinking.

Islamic Subjectivities and Critical Thinking: The Case of Shiite Madrasa-Alumni-Operated (SMA) Islamic Schools

Heterogeneity in the Karachi metropolis has also brought severe ethnic and sectarian rivalries and clashes in the last three decades. At the SMA Islamic school, when I met the principal, Mr. Habib, to talk about why his school followed the Montessori system, he was suspicious as to why I wanted to know more about a Shiite Islamic school. As a native observer, I did not lie but answered vaguely when Mr. Habib looked at me quizzically and asked, "Well, do you think that the links with religious traditions are the same as those of the Sunnis?" Instead, I stated that I tolerated the Sunni ways but that the Shiite pedagogies are different because a Shiite child grows up differently. Mr. Habib finally smiled in affirmation and said,

> That's right. We [pointing towards both of us] are different . . . Our mission at this school is to give an understanding of geography and social ethics with an understanding of the plurality of Islamic cultures in Pakistan. What is the location of Pakistan, how close is it to Iran, how the virtues of Hazrat Ali, peace be upon him [Prophet's cousin representing leadership of the Shiites], can help us learn about civic virtues . . . Where do you see madrasa teachers allowing self-directed activity to a child? We have a mission to impart Islamic knowledge in a way that teaches children to engage in critical but peaceful thinking right from the beginning.[2]

Mr. Habib's mission is to develop modern Shiite religious subjectivities in the students, as well as national subjectivities that interpret the modern Pakistani Islamic identity as a pluralistic one, in which Shiite religious historical figures inform civil responsibilities and politics. The Montessori activities and Mr. Habib's description of the school pedagogies further highlight that there is nothing monolithic about the Islamic tradition that defines religious curriculum. Nor is there any similarity in the kinds of religious subjectivity each of these schools create. However, the schools' patrons are similar in their efforts to engage in modern debates about active citizenry through the celebration of their Islamic schools of thought.

Sitting in on a Montessori class at the SMA Islamic school, I observed the Montessori directress, Ms. Kiran, begin an activity with four big boxes wrapped in bright colors. She loudly explained the task to the class of ten three- to five-year-olds. They would each get four cards and would need to look at them carefully and put them in the right box. One box was for pictures of plants, another for flowers, the third for cards of blue, red, and yellow colors, and the fourth box was wrapped with green inside with the picture of a mosque drawn in the center. The children were busy moving back and forth, putting one card in a box at a time. I took a spot next to the green box, in which children put in cards that said *Muhammad, Fatima, Ali, Hasan, Husayn*, and *the Quran*. The activity was emblematic of the visual, sensory, and analytical methods that the SMA Islamic school principal proudly described to me as characteristic of his school's unique Montessori system.

Ms. Kiran, the Montessori directress at the SMA school, explained the significance of Montessori at an Islamic school: "I combine my artistic skills and training in child psychology to develop posters, games, group exercises, word and object learning activities, passing on knowledge about living plants, animals, natural resources." I mentioned that I had noticed that each activity mentioned Prophet Muhammad's life. Ms. Kiran responded, "Exactly. The training in Islamic thinking needs to be given from the beginning. Only when a student knows about the sacrifices of Hazrat [honorable] Ali to continue the teachings of the prophet of Islam will they know how to preserve their Islamic tradition in times of turmoil."[3]

What I found unique about the activity was the way teachers followed their school's mission of developing cognitive abilities to identify and organize plants, colors, and flowers, along with their ability to recognize and classify Muslim and, in particular, Shiite personalities. The SMA Islamic school's pedagogical example analyzes the notion that religious institutions only create religious subjectivities in the students and that such a subjectivity is the same in all religious institutions. Unknown inside madrasas, such activities inside the SMA

Islamic schools create a religious subjectivity in children that complements their critical skills and knowledge in other subjects. Furthermore, the incorporation of knowledge about Shiite spiritual leaders at the school highlights that the religious subjectivities in Islamic schools are constructed in conformity with the sectarian traditions of school producers and patrons of knowledge.

A parent, Mr. Latif, whose son goes to the SMA Islamic school Montessori, spoke to me about his schooling choice. "The kindergarten system is not much cheaper than Montessori. Plus, in Montessori, children develop their cognitive capacities as well as what makes Ahle-Tashi [Twelver Shiites] different." I asked him if his son would complete his education up to tenth grade from the same school. He replied,

> Montessori education here is cheaper than in regular [private secular] schools. Plus, the environment is secure, and he will learn a thing or two about our faith [read sect]. I may transfer him after fifth grade to a different school [private secular] under Shiite administration. I haven't decided yet. I like the fact that they put high emphasis on the physical activity of the students here.[4]

Mr. Latif's educational choice shows how an Islamic school's Montessori is often an economical choice for parents. Whether the Islamic education is limited to *nazira* or includes *hifz*, the foundational courses for both are completed before beginning secondary school. Parents like Mr. Latif, therefore, find Islamic schools an alternative to the private secular schools because there a child can receive basic education in an Islamic environment, which can mold his moral subjectivity in such ways that, even when he is transferred to a secular school, he has the required knowledge to expand on his Islamic education in his family's sectarian tradition. Moreover, with no standardization of private secular schools, the majority of affordable schools lack space and teachers for physical training. As a result, schools in which physical fitness is part of the daily and weekly schedule are highly regarded by Karachi parents. The Shiite Islamic school is a financial deal for Mr. Latif, and his child's cognitive and physical health are nourished and his family's Shiite identity is kept alive.

1b) Creating Islamic Subjectivities: Primary and Secondary Educational Programs in Islamic Schools

The typical learning structure at Islamic schools is as follows: Students finish Montessori and in the first grade they start reading the Quran (*nazira*) along with education in secular subjects, such as math, English, Urdu, and science. In some schools, students have memorized ten out of thirty chapters of the Quran by the end of second grade. By the end of third grade, they have memorized twenty chapters, and by the end of the fifth, or last, grade of primary schooling, they have completely memorized the holy book. At the secondary school level (grades 6–10), students repeat the Quran and learn more intensive theological subjects, such as *tajvid*, *tafsir*, traditions of Sunna and the history of Islam. Computer education also begins at the secondary school level. I asked Qari Mohammad, owner of a JIMA Islamic school, why his school chose to make the students *huffaz* (people who have memorized the Quran) at the primary level. He responded,

> Because this is the time when memory is at its sharpest. When they are at the secondary level, they are more mature to understand the Quran. Their memory is not as perfect at that age, and their secular studies are getting harder. Right from the seventh grade, teachers start orienting them toward the O-level exams that they take in the ninth and tenth grades . . . besides, if students begin *hifz* at an early age, they grow up with a respect for religion and a sense of responsibility that they have memorized something very important that they must preserve for the rest of their lives.[5]

Contrary to the Islamic subjectivities that madrasa administrators seek to create, which enable their graduates fit to be employed only at other madrasas and mosques, Islamic school administrators like Qari Mohammad understand that their students' ultimate goal is to become professionals in various fields.

i) Islamic Appearance

Gender-segregation policies vary across Islamic school, depending on the intensity with which modern education is imparted in an Islamic environment. Thus, in some Islamic schools, gender segregation starts at the primary level (grades 1–5) and at some not until the secondary level (grades 6–10). In the more puritanical schools, usually those opened by madrasa alumni, both female students and faculty must follow strict purdah, and teachers must wear abaya. The administration stresses that veiling be observed not only as part of the in-school code of conduct but also during the after-school hours so that "piety" can become a way of life for female students. On the other hand, in Islamic schools more similar to private secular schools, gender segregation is often not there at the primary level. At the secondary level, boys and girls may sit in the same room, but at two ends of the class or in separate rows.

When appointing faculty and staff, whether for secular or religious subjects, it is customary for the administration to evaluate an applicant's religiosity so that teachers exemplify the parochial aspect of the school. Before such policies make one conclude that the Islamic environment in these schools is repressive for female teachers, it is important to note how the faculty regards these schools as vehicles for women to become independent professionals. Ms. Zareen, the Montessori directress at C1, talked to me about what guided her choice to teach at an Islamic school. "No other profession was allowed. My mother said that teaching would be okay. My father remained hesitant. So I went into the Montessori training centers. When you become a Montessori directress, the institute is responsible for finding you an internship. So here I am." I mentioned the strict veiling rules for the teachers. Ms. Zareen smiled. "I am the only one in my house like this. No one in my family observes purdah." I asked if that meant that she likes teaching at an Islamic school. Ms. Zareen replied, "The behavior of the administration is good, but our salaries are so low. Whenever we mention it, they say the school isn't doing so well. Sometimes I get the salary after two months. My family routinely asks me if I do 'welfare work!'" We both laughed.[6]

Maheen, a seventh grader at an SMA Islamic school and whose sister studies in fifth grade in the same school, said the following regarding the Islamic uniform at the school.

> I did primary schooling from Habib Girls School [a private secular school under Shiite administration, but one that operates like a secular school]. There, we covered our heads in the morning assembly during *qirat* only [qirat, recitation of a Quranic passage, is performed at the

beginning of the day in all schools]. When I came for admission here, I was wearing jeans and shirt. Now, I come in *kameez shalwar* and scarf, even on a non-uniform day. You are instantly noticeable when you don't dress modestly.

I asked Maheen how it was at home. She said, "My father is lenient, but my mother, my sister, and I all cover our heads when our relatives and friends come. Our principal says that even when we are at a personal gathering, we represent the school."[7]

Maheen's father spoke to me about his perspective on the issue. He said,

> See, morality is not in the dress. It is inside you. I like the fact that the school asks the students to dress modestly all the time. It does not have to be the scarf, but, if you don't get in the habit of dressing modestly as a child, it is harder to adjust to Islamic dress later on. You know, when it comes to girls, they have to adjust. I don't force anything on my girls. However, it is a fact that if I will tell them at the age of twenty that they dress a certain way, or if they were to get married in a family that is particular about it, it will be difficult to convince them when they are older to change their way of dressing. So it is good to be enculturated right from the beginning.[8]

ii) Islamic School Morning Assembly

Although Islamic schools operate under the same regulations as private secular schools, they distinguish their pedagogies from the latter by incorporating Islamic education in the school routine. The morning assembly is an example. In September 2007, I walked into an Islamic school in Karachi at 7:50 AM. The traffic outside had virtually disappeared. Two minutes before 8:00, head teachers stood in a row and students in all grades made lines facing them, standing in shortest-to-tallest order. Other teachers stood in a row behind the head teachers. Student assistants, class monitors, and prefects stood at attention on all four sides of the class lines. This assembly is typical of all public and private schools. However, the teaching lineup was unique in that madrasa graduates, who are teachers for *hifz* and *nazira*, stood right next to each other, a sight unknown in private secular schools. Teachers for secular subjects observed veiling and the entire school represented similar religiosity in appearance, except for the nursery-level students.

Two students from the secondary classes stood on either side of the national flag on the right. A microphone was placed at the center. After the assembly was formed, the physical trainer, commonly referred to as the PT teacher, came up to the microphone and instructed students in light exercises, consisting of stomping their feet, clapping their hands above their heads, and then turning in unison.[9] Formulaic exercises of this kind, often performed in a drill-like fashion, are also common in private secular school. However, due to gender-segregation rules and a restriction of girls not exercising in front of boys, the PT teachers at girls' Islamic school are always women.

After some physical exercise, students stand at attention while teachers and students review the latest news headlines and make important school announcements. This is followed by Quranic recitation with translation in Urdu, either in the form of long passages or several short passages. Compared to the practice in private secular schools, where Quranic recitation is a short formality to begin the day, at Islamic schools, such recitation is a means of measuring the student's ability in *din*. Recitation competitions are arranged, and students are awarded prizes and, in some instances, bonus points for secular subjects. At the SMA school and other Islamic schools, I noticed that the assembly runs longer, close to thirty minutes, than that at private secular schools, usually twenty minutes, due to Quranic recitation. The recitations not only reinforce the Islamic mission of the school but also provide secondary school students an audience to practice their recitation and memorization skills. Additional elements may be added to Quranic recitation in Islamic schools, depending on the school's sectarian tradition, something I will discuss later in this chapter.

iii) The Prayer Ritual: Creating "Muslimness"
On a breezy day in March, I had an appointment with Ms. Majida, the vice principal of the girls' branch of a JIMA Islamic school. The classes were downstairs, and I was taken upstairs to one of the office rooms next to a large terrace area. I asked Ms. Majida what need Islamic education at an Islamic school could fulfill that Islamiat at a private secular school could not. She asked, "Do they stop for prayers at other private [secular] schools? Have you seen them notice when they hear the prayer call from the nearby mosque?"

I gestured in the negative.

Then they don't have Islamiat. What is Islamiat? Teaching about Islam. They have a math period during *zuhr* [afternoon prayer] and then in the Islamiat period, they teach about the principles of *din*. Islamiat is Islamiat only when it becomes a way of life. In a half hour, you will see how the whole school gathers here when they hear the call for prayers.

Ms. Majida then pointed toward the large terrace and said, "You are welcome to join."[10]

Indeed, in another fifteen minutes, staff women took out big rugs and mats from the attic and laid them out. In another few minutes, the call for prayers began, and grades 4–10 climbed the stairs in lines. Everyone removed their shoes and took their place on the mats. The faculty and administrative staff stood in the front rows, and the students stood behind them. I was gestured to join the teachers' row. The *hifz* teacher, Ms. Qamrunissa, led the prayers. As the prayer break ended, students proceeded to their science, English, and math classes. This is where the religious universe of Islamic schools is so different from that of the madrasas. The social universe, at the same time, is also different from that of private secular and public secular schools in the way Quranic recitation in the morning assembly and noon prayers are integrated into the school routine. At public and private schools, there is no prayer room or prayer breaks observed, and children are not allowed to leave the class to pray. Conversely, I saw at eight different Islamic schools that classes break for thirty minutes for the *zuhr* prayer in courtyards, covered halls, or terrace areas designated for congregation. Students and staff go to their separate ablution areas. Such features bring some Islamic schools architecturally closer to madrasas. Such organized prayer breaks, in which sectarian prayer traditions are followed, create Islamic subjectivities in the students in a modern educational environment.

iv) Islamiat and Islamic Learning

In the month of August, as I sat in on the first Islamiat period in grade 6 at the beginning of a new school year at a JIMA Islamic school, the first question that the head teacher asked the students was, "How did you spend your summer holidays?" Some children gave embarrassed looks, trying to recall one significant activity that the teacher would applaud. Others mentioned going to other cities to meet relatives. A few began pulling their summer homework copies out of their bags. The teacher then asked them to take their textbooks out and asked a boy to read what was a part of *Surat al-Baqara* [longest chapter of the Quran]. Two more students read fluently and with proper Arabic pronunciation. The teacher murmured, "*Jazak Allah* [May Allah reward you]." The first student gave a half smile and sat down. When the second student heard the greeting, she responded, "*Jazak Allah Khayran* [May Allah reward you generously]." The teacher gave a pleased look on hearing an Islamic response greeting. The third student picked it up, waited for the teacher's murmur, and instantly responded in a similar manner. Then she began quizzing them on the questions. "You should all have your hands raised. You should remember it. We have done it before." Then the teacher looked at me with hesitation, as if in a job interview, and asked one of the brainy girls, Tehzeeb, to translate the portion of the Quran. She got half of it correct. "I want you all to get one thing straight. This is for everyone. Islamiat is not like other subjects. You finish a book with a teacher, give it to your younger brother," she paused to watch the children muse, "and have a good summer, forgetting everything you learned in class then come again with new books." She then asked, "What makes us a true Muslim?" This one seemed easier, and the students warmed to the subject. Several raised their hands, and the teacher chose a slender girl in the third row this time, who answered, "When we practice Islamic knowledge in our everyday lives."

"Yes", the teacher said. "Two things, remember? *Huququl-ibad* [working for the rights of humanity] and ilm [knowledge], the first message given to Muhammad, peace be upon him, by angel Gabriel, peace be upon him."[11]

After the class was over, the teacher told me that it is the school's policy to begin a new session with that question in order to find out whether religious ideas are reinforced at home during the summer months.

> I have to revise more than the other teachers. It is usual for parents to send children to our school and think that they will get all the Islamic instruction. If education at our madrasas was coupled with proper

Islamic practice, madrasa students would have chosen the path of peace, not violence. Islamic education is not something in a capsule form that students can pop in and move on. Then, when children leave for home or go on vacation, they watch TV, party, play computer and video games all day, stop praying and do not revise their Quran, because of which they face difficulty continuing the memorization from where they left. I emphasize the need to students and their parents as much as I can. The rest is up to the family.

She summed up by quoting Prophet Muhammad with a smile, "There is no compulsion in religion"[12]

During the break at the JIMA Islamic school, I asked Tania from the sixth-grade class I sat in on earlier if she thought that the Quranic lesson the teacher taught that day was too hard to retain. Tania replied, "Nobody remembers it the first day. Not even the kids who already know the translation and how to read from prior training. I'll go home, sit with my dad, read it a few times, remember the translation, go through the questions, and I'll be prepared." I then spotted Tehzeeb, the smart girl who had translated the Quran in class. While we ate our chips and sandwiches, I asked her if she had received religious training prior to joining this school. Tehzeeb answered, "No. My tuition miss [teacher] helps me." I asked her if she was her Islamiat tutor. Tehzeeb casually replied, "All subjects. I do homework with her every day. I just practice Quran in front of her after we finish the homework. My mother tells me to do that even if there is no Islamiat homework, so that I don't forget the proper pronunciation."[13]

I asked the principal of the JIMA school why additional Islamic instruction was needed when all private secular schools already have Islamiat as a required course. He replied, "Merely studying Islam as a subject in the curriculum does not motivate a child to grow up to become a faithful believer and a good citizen. Alluding to Prophet Muhammad's saying about Islam, he then elaborated,

> Islam must be taught as a complete code of life. Our school strives not to make children read extra books on Islam, but to incorporate Islam in their everyday lives and social dealings. We want to make sure that they learn the kind of Islam that they cannot leave at the school gate at the end of the day, as you see in private secular schools. We want to teach them the Islam that they can take home.[14]

Mr. Kareem, father of sixth grader Tania, explained to me why it is important to rejuvenate faith through education.

> Western materialism and the Western media-propagated modernity pose a big threat to the traditional values and culture of Pakistan. It is not possible to impart nominal Islamic teaching and secular education and expect that an educated mind will be able to counter these vices. Children must live in a religious environment and have a commitment to religious duties from the age of five.[15]

The narratives of Islamic schools' administrators, teachers, students, and their parents highlight how the schools are vigilant about ensuring that the children do not treat Islam as a codified subject, but rather as a way of life. This mission is strengthened in the face of materialism and the Western media's representation of modernity that poses a threat to the Pakistani culture and to the Muslim *ummah*.

I joined the morning assembly at an Islamic school located in the lower-middle-class neighborhood of Lyari. A student came up to the microphone and recited a *sura* (chapter) of the Quran. Students lined up by grades in neat rows stopped fidgeting. All girls, dressed in scarves, dropped their heads solemnly. The boys quickly put on their caps, folded their arms around their waists, and looked down, waiting for the boy to start. A fifth grader had an ongoing joke with a fourth grader standing across from him, who winked at him. The prayer began, the fifth grader giggled and was about to wink back when the fourth grader froze. The fifth grader caught on that the teacher had noticed. The recitation ended, and the classes returned to their rooms. When the fifth graders had settled and taken out their English textbooks, the teacher called the boy to the front of the class and scolded him, asking him what face he would show to Allah on the Judgment Day and telling him how badly he had reflected on his family by giggling at the time of prayer. The boy first listened, then meekly complained that Mona, Asfia, and Kiran had also been talking in front of the girls' line. The teacher told him to stand outside the class. I watched him as the rest of the class began writing about the five things they would do after school using phrases in their textbooks. Twenty-five minutes into class, the boy was let back in.

As the teacher's scolding highlights, the boys' religious subjectivities are constructed in an atmosphere in which negligence of religious education is equated with dishonoring one's family. What stayed with the boy as he was allowed into the class was the shame of being thrown out of the class in front of his classmates. Nobody in the class made eye contact with him after he returned to his desk. The *nazira* teacher, whose period was next, informed the students that she had learned about the boy's folly and that she was disappointed about how he had made light of Allah's words. The boy had his head sunk the entire time and barely looked into the textbook to read the *sura* that the teacher began explaining. She then asked students to stand and recite it one by one. She skipped the boy.

In the English and *nazira* classes, I saw students make mistakes and ask questions. This pedagogical practice stands in stark contrast to the submissive and passive manner in which *nazira* is taught in madrasas. The teachers were accommodating and gave good explanations in such instances. However, it is not just what is studied in class, but more so the students' attitude toward being in an Islamic educational environment that informs their religious subjectivities. Like the private secular schools, the pedagogical environment in Islamic schools ensures quality education in a participatory atmosphere. However, in addition, the students who let Islamic education pass as routine are treated like outcasts, thereby creating a responsibility and guilt in them that, unlike the students in private secular schools who may forget Islamiat once they graduate from the school, can remain an integral part of their moral subjectivity.[16]

v) Islamic Education through Cognition
Not only in the international sphere but also inside Pakistan, the image of a madrasa and its teachings have come to symbolize the most conservative, intolerant, and extremist Muslims. It has also homogenized the ways in which Western media and scholarship have presented Islamic practice and education. The producers of knowledge and patrons at Islamic schools are trying to carve out an Islamic subjectivity that is recognized as traditional, but at the same time modern and moderate. At C1 Islamic school, I sat in the *nazira* class, where the teacher, Ms. Ayesha, read out a few Quranic verses from the textbook, then told the students to see if they could break them down and write

the meaning in Urdu on their own. As some students highlighted familiar words and others scribbled, she checked everyone's progress, while complimenting them for their efforts. Next, she randomly chose students to tell her one word of which they knew the meaning. She then put the words, transitions, and prepositions that the students were not familiar with on the blackboard. She read them out, and the students repeated in a chorus. Ms. Ayesha then explained their meanings and asked students to volunteer to tell the meaning of a complete verse. The environment in the class was interactive and relaxed.[17]

I visited a madrasa in Federal B Area, a lower- to middle-class area of Karachi. I saw children between the ages of nine and thirteen reciting the Quran fluently and replacing familiar Urdu vocabulary with trained Arabic accents. When the period was over, I sat with a group from the class and asked a student to read from the Urdu textbook I had with me. Urdu and Arabic share the same script. However, the child was unable to read it. I asked several students after him, and they failed to read the book as well. I showed how each letter had formed the word and pointed out the words that were Arabic in origin. The children still could not do the reading. It turned out that the children could read Arabic rather than Urdu, not because they understood the former more than the latter, but because they had memorized the visual style of each of the words in the Quran. The first few times, students hear the teacher read it. Then, by daily and sometimes hourly repetition, they learn what the word should sound like based on how it looks and reads.[18] While that may not be the case in all Pakistani madrasas, that pedagogical style informs the way Islamic education and theology students are conceived in scholarship. Islamic schools remind us to adopt a bottom-up approach and understand Pakistani Islamic subjectivities created through schooling as diverse and in relation to the modern social, class, and professional concerns of their consumers.

My experience in Ms. Ayesha's class and other C1 classes was different in that I did not find students attempting memorization without engaging their cognitive faculties. Students become *hafiz al-Quran* only after acquiring proficiency in *nazira* in which they understand what they read. This practice makes Islamic schools a unique religious education in contrast to the madrasas, upon which the Musharraf government cracked down, because the government claimed that the students read Quranic script without understanding it and memorize the meaning that their teachers want them to believe.[19]

After class, I complimented Ms. Ayesha for encouraging the translation of words and phrases and for allowing the students to ask about what they read. She replied,

> See, this is *din* . . . they should be able to understand it without the teacher . . . we are here for guidance, but this knowledge is Allah's blessing and his blessings are equal for everyone. You and I can't put a cap on them and decide how much the flow should be. I encourage my students to do extra readings . . . to build their own collection of *tafsir* [exegesis]. This is *sadqa-e-jaaria* [sacrifice in the name of humanity] . . . Islamic learning in our school is democratic. We think of the students as individuals with free minds. We allow them to think what they are about to believe in. Without that, learning about Islam is no good. Look at the madrasas. They produce scholars in the eyes of the world. If they really understand what they are reading, would they become terrorists?

I shook my head in negation. "A *nazira* class is not just *nazira*. Children can ask the *maulana [religious teacher] saab* [sahib, polite manner of addressing] questions. It's a discussion forum, not a forced imprisonment for children."[20] Teachers like Ms. Ayesha, following their Islamic schools' mission, seek to develop a religious subjectivity in their students in which faith is based on cognition. In this way, she and others are promoting an Islamic schooling that brings down the binary opposition between the sacred and the temporal by advocating self-understanding and judgment of Quranic texts. Speaking to an eighth grader, Huma, later that day at Ms. Ayesha's C1 school, I asked about such pedagogy. Huma responded, "When we read and understand Quran right in grades 5, 6, 7, 8, we know the translation of words and phrases. Then we don't just read. We stop to understand them. It's funny because now, I read Quran slower than before because my mind is involved!"[21] Huma's mother recounted a story in relation to Huma's observation.

> Once we were at a Quran Khwaani and Huma was the last one to finish the *para* [one of the thirty portions in which the Quran is divided and read at gatherings]. She was teased by relatives, saying that she was in

an Islamic school and it should be a piece of cake for her. You see, people don't understand. They think speed is everything. It is important, but only as long as you understand what you are reading. I discussed it with the *hifz* teacher. She said that Huma is still in the transitional stage. First comes the pronunciation, then the understanding, then the speed. "Inshallah, she will read better and faster than you do."[22]

Huma's mother's comment stands in contrast to the rote memorization strategy employed for Islamic education at the madrasas. As I mentioned in chapter 3, madrasa students memorize pronunciation of words without knowing what they are reading. They are, therefore, speedy "readers," but do not relate to the Islamic education they receive. Instead, their primary relation is with the ideology of their teachers.[23] The *hidden curriculum* of madrasas leads to the radicalization of the students and a narrow worldview in which Islamic education is not accompanied by reason and rationality.[24] Unlike the madrasas, where students follow their teachers' theological interpretation until they have themselves become religious scholars, education in Islamic schools does not create a hierarchy in religious scholarship. The statements of Ms. Ayesha, Huma, and Huma's mother seem to highlight that each student is free to understand the meaning of Islamic education using individual cognition and directly engage with his or her Islamic tradition. Islamic schools highlight Eickelman's assertion that Islamic tradition is modernized when people treat it objectively, ask questions concerning their relationship to it, and reconceptualize it, thereby taking the religious tradition away from the traditional hierarchical authority of theologians and closer to the experiences of the masses.[25] Ms. Ayesha's and Huma's assessments of Islamic education seem to point to a Muslim subjectivity in which students are lent authority to use their own cognitive and analytical skills to understand the place of Islamic tradition in their lives.

vi) Music in Islamic schools
In many of the private secular schools, music and art classes are part of the weekly schedule. In the Islamic schools, music is almost nonexistent. Musical instruments are rarely used because of a commonly held conception that they are not Islamic. Bilal ibn Riyah was the first official *muezzin* (the person at the mosque who calls people for prayers) of Islam

appointed by Prophet Muhammad. He was an Ethiopian slave freed by the prophet's companion and is known for his beautiful voice. An administrator at a madrasa-alumni-operated Islamic school that follows the O-level curriculum and examination system described his school's approach toward music and related Bilal ibn Riyah's story to me.

> See, Bilal had a beautiful voice, but only when he used it to call people toward Allah did it make him famous. And look how using musicality to pass on the divine message made Bilal, whom everyone in Arabia considered of inferior birth, the closest to the Prophet among all believers.[26]

Prophet Muhammad is said to have disliked the music and dancing that accompanied his arrival in Medina. Therefore, conservative theologians of the country consider music as un-Islamic. The majority of Islamic schools teach children nursery rhymes and poems without music or in a manner that only allows chorus singing. Thus, while private secular schools have a custom of assigning a music teacher to play the piano while children sing jingles, this practice does not exist in the majority of Islamic schools. Some Islamic schools allow drums to supply background beat to jingles with moral messages, an Arab custom at the time of the prophet that conservative theologians describe as the only form of music permissible in Islam. The Islamic schools mentioned above forbid music but allow the singing of *hamd* and naat with the accompaniment of a handheld drum. This practice highlights how Islamic school administrations redefine the O-level system of private secular schooling in the country by infusing it with Islamic moral code.

Ms. Darakhshan, parent of sixth-grader Zara, spoke to me about the music rule.

> Music is not allowed here, so that the students concentrate on learning. Even then, there is no stopping the playing with digital instruments. You see their cell phones ringing with all kinds of Indian film songs and Pakistani pop songs. One time, I asked my daughter playing with her mobile during the break to do something with the ringtone variety she had downloaded. She asked, "Are mobile tones also music?" . . . they have enough on their hands to keep them distracted from learning . . . it's good to see the text and music culture stop somewhere.[27]

I asked Hashim, a sixth grader, during the break whether he listens to music. When he said yes, I asked whether it was Pakistani pop or Indian film music. He said he listened to both and named his favorites in both countries. "Do you go out to purchase CDs and cassettes?" I asked.

Hashim replied, "Bhai [older brother] puts it on the computer. I listen to what he gets." I asked if he liked that musical instruments are absent in his school. Hashim instantly responded, "That is because it is an Islamic school. There is no music in the context of religion." I asked Hashim if he watched the high-demand Indian pirated movies shown by local cable service providers. Hashim replied, "My dad doesn't like it. Sometimes my mother and sister put them on. Sometimes Bhai gets action films that I watch with him. But he doesn't allow me to watch the romantic ones." I asked him if Bhai still watches them. Blushing, Hashim said, "Yeah."[28]

Hashim's experience of music is similar to his brother's experience of watching films. Foreign films are considered un-Islamic, just as music is. Hashim has developed a particular kind of subjectivity with regard to music—one that allows him to discern the contexts and environments, where it is and isn't appropriate. Unlike the dormitory-style life of a madrasa student, the fact that Islamic education is packaged for school hours only allows Hashim to change what Islamic behavior entails at home. It is in such experiences that even in the same Islamic institution, religious messages are not received passively or homogeneously by students, but rather in relation to the demands and aspirations of their social lives.

vii) Art in Islamic Schools

In Islamic schools, art has come to mean calligraphy, because Muslims are not allowed to draw human figures that can be equated with idols. Ms. Nadia, administrator at the C2 school, discussed the activity: "Girls are much calmer and precise when they draw and paint. For the boys, art is more like therapy. When they are busy doing it, they do not think about boxing and wrestling and all that crap they want to try out in school."[29]

To get the teacher's perspective, I spoke to the Montessori directress, Ms. Mahawash, who told me about her own background in fine arts.

> I got a diploma from the Karachi School of Arts. I think that I can make use of my art here. I applied to other schools. They would tell

me to teach English, Urdu, math, as well in the same salary, and the emphasis on art was minimal. I chose this place because I only wanted to be an art teacher. Here, there is a regular art period and supplies. I just like all kinds of arts and crafts. They do art in the Islamic spirit here. I don't think it is wrong. In fact, being here has inspired me to do calligraphy, abstract, and nature art instead of just drawing caricatures of people, which is more inspirational and correct.[30]

viii) Producing Religious Subjectivity through Language
In private secular schools, educational prestige is communicated through strict policies on the use of English at all times. This is also true in terms of greetings. Students must wish their teachers "good morning" and "good afternoon" when they see them. Islamic schools, on the other hand, enforce English as the medium of instruction and communication but add to this social prestige a religious flavor by implementing an only-Islamic greetings policy. Teachers continuously emphasize, for example, that students, upon entering or leaving a room or meeting someone, should never say "hello," "good morning," or "good-bye" but should use the correct, Arabic, religious salutation, assalamoaleikum (peace be upon you). To reinforce this, teachers punish any child who carelessly blurts out an English greeting in lieu of a correct Islamic one by executing an old familiar punishment in all schools, that of telling the student to become a *murgha* (rooster). The student is supposed to catch and hold his ears by passing his hands through his bent legs. While such a subhuman punishment from the teacher is common in schools—just as parents casually spanking a child at home is not considered abuse—in this case, it reminds the student of the demoralizing consequences of blindly following Western culture, conveying the school's message that Western education is simply an instrument to achieve worldly success, not a way of life. At other times, punishments may include standing outside the classroom for one or more periods. A more common punishment is a teacher's verbal taunting. As I came out of a classroom with fifth-grade students at C1, a girl looked up, saw a teacher, and said, "Good morning."

The teacher nodded in response, then quietly took her aside and asked, "Are you a Muslim?"

The girl nodded.

"Then why can't you greet in your own language?"

"Sorry, ma'am," the girl said.

"Child, it is good that you know how to say it in English, but Allah has blessed us with such a beautiful greeting—*salaam*—the message of peace. We shouldn't be embarrassed to say it."[31]

This conversation, occurring at Islamic schools offering O-level-style education, points to how the school simultaneously creates class and religious subjectivities in the students using English and Arabic. Besides being able to read the Arabic script and a few words in greetings that are similar in Urdu, Pakistanis do not understand Arabic. Islamic schools teachers are well aware of these limitations and only emphasize Arabic/Islamic greetings that are closer in spelling and pronunciation to Urdu. For example, *subh bakhayr* (good morning) in Urdu, because it is very close to *sabah al-khayr* (good morning) in Arabic, is replaced by the Arabic version. However, *ilalliqa*, Arabic for *good-bye* is different from Allah hafiz in Urdu and therefore the latter is maintained. Instead, *Allah hafiz* has replaced *Khuda hafiz* in roughly the last decade, as a result of a Wahabi campaign that holds that *Khuda*, Persian for Allah, does not completely convey the oneness of Allah.[32] By contrast, in the case of the private secular schools, rarely can one find a student greeting in Urdu and never in Arabic. "Good morning" and "good afternoon" and other greetings in English, instead, communicate that the school is preparing students for higher social status and successful professional lives.

In the private secular schools, it is common for a class to applaud a student's achievement. At Islamic schools, applause is forbidden. The correct way of rewarding a child is to invoke the name of God, because he alone deserves all praise. Thus, students learn to say, "*Jazak Allah*," "*Mashallah*," or "*Subhanallah* (glory be to Allah)." The inclusion of religious greetings in Arabic language, while speaking in Urdu and English, inflects students' moral and social subjectivities. Arabic is a feature in Islamic schools that differentiates the British O-level education of Islamic schools from those of the private secular schools. In private secular schools, the prestige attached to the British system is emphasized by obligating students to speak and greet in English only and failing to do so may result in punishment. In Islamic schools, however, the Islamic aspect of the prestigious, foreign education is emphasized through Arabic and affects students by engendering the importance of incorporating the language of Islam, more than the English language, into their social life.

Inside Islamic school classrooms, it is common for teachers to use a distinctly Islamic language to express emotions and gratitude. In one case, at an Islamic school catering to a lower-middle-class neighborhood of Federal B Area, I sat in on the sixth-grade Urdu class. The teacher saw a student without a pencil borrow one from his friend. He said "thank you" to him in English, and the teacher stared at him. "Do you want to be sent to the principal's office?"

He said, "Sorry, Teacher," and turned to the boy to say, "*Jazak Allah* [may Allah reward you for the good]."[33]

Later that day, I mentioned to the principal at the same Islamic school that a sixth grader got in trouble and was sent to his office. He instantly interjected.

> The warnings are just to warn the children that there are consequences. Didn't you get warnings when you were in school? Don't you think you learned something from them? It's not just the madrasas. The beating, the punishment, everything goes on in other private [secular] schools, too. I regularly survey classrooms to ensure that no teacher is resorting to physical punishment . . . but warnings are necessary, because at the regular [secular] private schools, there is no punishment for neglect of religion . . . no consequences if you do not carry yourself in a proper Islamic manner, forget the words of Allah . . . why do we view nonreligious and Islamic knowledge through a different lens? They must be seen in the same light and taught with the same strictness.[34]

It was common for Islamic school administrators who knew I was comparing their schools to private secular schools and madrasas to mention other kinds of schools and to highlight the assets of their schools. The principal's narrative was interesting because he promoted his school as a place where one is accountable, not only for the Islamic subjects taught, but also for conducting themselves in an Islamic way in speech and action. It is true that physical punishment is common in private secular schools. The principal is, however, careful about not turning Islamic discipline into extremist Islamic education.

ix) The Latecomers in Islamic Schools and the Production of Religious Subjectivity in Class Education

I sat in on a ninth-grade Islamiat class at C1. The teacher saw a student, Arsalan, talking during her lecture. She turned and said, "I will send you to the principal's office." Being a product of a private school in Karachi, I knew that the warning implied that the student could be beaten in private in the principal's office for his mischief and that there was the prospect of the humiliation of one's parents being called to school.

The student instantly began pleading in English, "I'm sorry, Teacher, I won't do it again." He continued incessantly in the same rhythm for a few minutes until his voice faded away. The class sat in silence, trying to predict whether he would be saved. It was a moment that made me forget why I was in the class and turned me into that native who could not recognize the difference between the observer and the observed. I made guesses about the boy's fate, wondering if standing in the back of the class would be better than a whipping in the principal's office.

To my surprise, the teacher turned toward him, reconsidered her verdict, and said, "Allah does not have a place in heaven for those who talk too much. Your prayers are not going to be answered if you accompany them with this kind of behavior. She then pronounced a penance of writing the lines: "I'll not talk in class again. Ya Allah! I promise I will not disappoint you again," two hundred times.[35]

Punishments of this sort are customary. However, the nature of the punishment at C1, which coerced the boy into feeling guilty not by reference to the teacher, principal, or the school, but instead, to Allah, was unique. Nonadherence to the teacher's orders is equated with being distanced from Allah. The teacher's authority is maintained, similar to what I observed in private secular schools and from my own experience studying in one, but the manner in which it is maintained, by making the student pay for his bad conduct by writing penances to the higher authority of Allah, is unique to Islamic schools.

After school, I met Arsalan and told him how I could relate to what happened in class. He looked at me sullenly. "I'm just waiting to get done with school. Once I'm in high school, I'll do whatever I want." I asked him if he would go to an Islamic high school. "Of course not! I'll go to a public school." I commented that the A-level/intermediate studies were so much more difficult than O-levels. "Yes, but I know I can do it because I won't have all these extra subjects that I have to pass. O-levels is hard enough, and then to have to deal with extra *hifz*, *nazira* and Islamiat courses! Once I'm out of this school, I'll be free. My dad is also thinking about getting me into one of the A-level [private high] schools. Ah," he mused, daydreaming. "Those A-level schools are so modern and so liberal! Students do stage and drama, have their own pop bands . . . it would be perfect . . . but if I can't get in, then a public college [high school] would be would be good, too. I can't wait!"[36]

Arsalan's perspective is similar to that of other sixteen-year-old in any private school in Pakistan who craves to leave the tight discipline and structure of school life and go to high school/intermediate college. He dreams about the college environment as not just a disciplinary escape but also an escape from the Islamic education that he did not identify with, even after reaching the O-level exam. An A-level college is far more expensive and selective than the O-level. As a middle-class boy going to an Islamic school in his neighborhood, Arsalan's understood the environment at an A-level college to be one in which the elite culture of the school would allow him to explore his talents in music and drama, ways that are contrary to the ideology of the Islamic school he will graduate from.

Arsalan's narrative highlights Paul Willis's argument that the subjectivities created through the schooling process are not only a result of the school's mission but of students deliberately resisting and adopting certain subjectivities.[37] Moreover, similar to Bourdieu and Passeron's argument, educational subjectivities are formed as a result of the interaction among the school's ideology, the teaching and disciplining methodologies, and the aptitudes, family backgrounds, and aspirations of the students.[38]

Parent Perspective

I asked Arsalan to introduce me to his mom, promising him that I would not tell her about the episode in class. He arranged for his mom to come after school one day. I asked her why Arsalan went to a private Islamic instead of a private secular school.

> He used to go to a regular [private secular] school. His dad [typically, wives in Pakistan do not refer to their husbands by their names] became more religious. Once Arsalan was done with primary school, his dad decided to transfer him to an Islamic school. He doesn't like it here . . . maybe if he had gone to this school from the nursery stage, he would've adjusted better.

I asked her if she thought the Islamic school had changed him. "I can't say much about that . . . or what environment he will seek as he goes on to the college level. I just care about his grades, and he got the third highest score in the O-level exams in his class [school]."[39]

Arsalan's case stands as an example of the students who are enrolled between the ages of eight and ten in Islamic schools. Sometimes they come from the madrasas, in which case, as I mentioned in chapter 3, they need to receive tutoring in secular education. However, in cases like that of Arsalan, the teachers, students, and their parents struggle to cultivate a new form of moral subjectivity in the student. Arsalan's middle-aged father is one of the several people I came to know who grew up during the 1980s Islamization and was drawn toward learning more about his faith in the post–9/11 and post-Musharraf madrasa crackdown environment. The example highlights the continuing efforts of Pakistani patrons in finding an educational discourse that conforms to the prestige and professional success guaranteed in the O-level education, that can continue the quality that the private secular schools were promoted for in the 1980s, and that can let madrasa education survive without its limitations.

x) Islamic Schools Textbooks: Creating Religious Subjectivities
I was looking for some home-based employment to support fieldwork expenses when I saw an advertisement for translators for textbooks. I made an appointment and visited the office. After completing the evaluation form, I was guided to the director's office, who explained that he wanted to introduce a new kind of textbook system in the market. The textbooks would infuse Islamic knowledge into the curricula for secular subjects. The meeting introduced me to a wide network of private publishing houses that have, in the last decade, begun publishing textbooks on secular subjects such as science, English, and social studies in which visuals, quotes, and additions at the end of the chapters are related to Islamic values with the subject. These new science textbooks for primary students tell them about different kinds of food, nutrition, health, and so forth by reminding them that cleanliness is important because it is the backbone of principles laid down by Allah and that the reason one is able to enjoy, distinguish, and achieve anything is because of Allah.[40]

Many private publishing houses have emerged that sell textbooks on Islamiat in English and on secular subjects after Islamizing their contents.

English lends prestige to the subject of Islamiat, and Islamizing secular subjects morally legitimizes modern education. These textbooks and reference books have wide appeal among immigrant, second-generation Pakistanis in the United States and the United Kingdom, who use them in Islamic schools or at home to develop a distinct sense of Islamic identity in their children. These Islamized books also have a wide market in the Islamic schools of Malaysia and Indonesia. In Pakistan, these books are the official textbooks in Islamic schools. Students are instructed at the beginning of every academic year to purchase them from designated retail bookstores. An important feature of these textbooks is integrating Islam and secular knowledge. To take the example of an Islamic school fifth-grade social studies textbook in English, students are told about the preindustrial age, when the barter system was followed and everyone's needs were met. The industrial age lead to high disparity between the haves and have-nots and people slaved on another's land. The textbook notes, "The poor in most of the cases are in debt which keeps on increasing because interest is added to the original sum of money."[41]

While up to this point, the lesson reads similar to a textbook at a private secular school, it is followed by an anecdote on Islam. The textbook shows men with beards and women in cloaks from the back, so that their faces are not visible accepting food from a bearded man in good clothes. The caption reads,

> It is not the Muslim way to exploit the poor. Hazrat [honorific title] Muhammad (PBUH) always laid special stress on paying the laborers fully and immediately . . . Paying *zakat* [alms] . . . is [the] basic duty of every Muslim . . . Helping the widows, the orphans, the sick and the poor is the greatest of virtues according to the teachings of Islam. We must try our best to follow it.[42]

Similarly, a science primary school textbook at an Islamic school shows parts of a human body. Something that is not seen in a private secular school textbook is the accompanying message: "Allah has given us a body."[43] Thus, blending secular knowledge with Islam is an essential feature of Islamic school teaching.

The kinds of textbooks that Islamic schools choose, whether they are contracted with private publishers or designed by the schools' own publishing houses, present an Islamic outlook to education by Islamicizing the narrative, illustrations, and quizzes. Additional text or footnotes at the end of the lesson (see the text mentioning *zakat* above) are consistently incorporated to relate and to validate the world of modern, secular knowledge with passages from the Quran, *hadith*, or a review of the Islamic way of life. A fifth-grade social studies textbook, for example, introduces students to evergreen, deciduous, and conifer trees. This is followed by a "Did You Know?" section that states, "Hazrat Muhammad said, 'Whosoever plants a tree, shall earn a house in paradise.'"[44]

Inside the C2 Islamic school, I noticed that school walls and notice boards carry quotes from the Quran and *hadith* that construct a visual and symbolic world around the students as they walk in and out of the assembly and class or go on breaks that constantly remind them of their Muslim identities. The schools construct a view that reinforces and synthesizes an Islamic worldview into the secular and modern educational experiences of the students. Thus, compatibility of Islam with secular knowledge is a main concern in Islamic schools pedagogies.

Not only is secular knowledge validated by Islamic injunctions in the Islamic school textbooks, but the Pakistani culture is also promoted by portraying it as synonymous to Islamic culture. In a social science textbook, the idea of family as a social unit is introduced with visuals of a three-generation Pakistani family sitting in a living room. A bubble shows a married woman looking at her father and thinking, "I love my parents." Another bubble shows a boy looking at this woman and thinking, "I love my parents."[45] The lesson ends with the line, "Family is a blessing of Allah." Family is the basic unit of a healthy society, and in Pakistan a child grows up with a collectivist rather than an individualistic ideal of self. The textbook promotes this collectivist ideal and teaches students that, to be considered a civil member of the society, caring for the wishes and needs of the family before personal needs and showing utmost loyalty to them at every stage of life is essential. Individualism is associated with the West, and, therefore, Western lifestyles are conceived as a cultural deterrent to the Pakistani social fabric. Promoting a collectivist subjectivity makes the social studies lesson Islamic.

Similarly, a national culture bound by an overarching Islamic identity is promoted in some Islamic school textbooks. What unites the people of all the four provinces and the Muslims of the disputed Kashmir territory is Islam. It reifies the two-nation theory, the idea that Pakistanis are a nation built in the name of Islam; when Pakistan was still a part of India, Muslims and Hindus were already two separate nations, and their separation was unavoidable.[46]

It is not to say that Pakistan studies, science, and social studies textbooks in public and private schools are strictly secular. Following Zia-ul-Haq's Islamization era, much of the secular curricula in public and private schools were Islamized and have remained largely neglected in revisions by the Ministry of Education. Even the Musharraf government, while coercing madrasas to incorporate modern education more rigorously, declared in the Educational Policy 1998–2010 that *nazira* Quran would be introduced as a compulsory component from grades 1–8, while at the secondary level translation of the selected verses from the Holy Quran would be offered. Since the 1980s, the history of the Indian subcontinent has been rewritten in textbooks to ignore all non-Islamic aspects of the country's history and to construct an Islamic past of Pakistan only.[47] Many of the textbooks used in Islamic schools are neither specially produced by private publishers for the schools nor published by the schools themselves. They are, especially at the secondary level, similar to those used in private secular and public schools. However, the books differ in that Islamic schools openly supplement secular knowledge with Islamic instruction and are not shy about imparting Islam in the traditional way because they seek to revive the madrasa tradition of pre-partition India where it prepared Muslims for both professional and spiritual excellence.

An excerpt from a brochure handed out to parents at a JIMA Islamic school informs them that in Islamic schools students are taught the virtue of courage by reference to Muslim history. The brochure contains the list of character and civil virtues taught in the school, which combines universal virtues like avoiding jealousy, being helpful, and so forth with the virtues that brings one closer to Allah, such as loving Prophet Muhammad, praying to Allah in trouble, and so on. The description of character under the heading "Islam and Character Education" explains how the school seeks to incorporate Muslim subjectivity in the students as they learn the meaning of belief, value, and character. Unlike private secular schools, where social studies textbooks discuss civil behavior by instructing children to observe state laws and to fulfill their political and social rights and duties, some Islamic schools distinguish themselves by instructing students to choose Prophet Muhammad as a role model and follow his life examples on how to behave positively and actively engage as community members. Similarly, the importance of cleanliness for a healthy life is told by instructing students to follow Prophet Muhammad's *uswa hasana* (excellent example of conduct).

A textbook on character education at a JIMA Islamic school lays out the essentials of a holistic personality: *iman* (faith), knowledge, and good deeds. Because Jamaat-e-Islami was a party founded by Sayyid Abul Ala Maudoodi in British India as a mode of achieving political power through peaceful means and boycott of Westernization, the JIMA Islamic school describes iman, the cornerstone of Muslim character, in the light of his teachings. In this way, Islamic values are incorporated with regard to the ideological affiliations of the entrepreneurs, and textbooks are designed accordingly. Islamic values depicted in this way highlight that civil virtues are not incompatible with Islam, such as in the exercise of intellect (*aql*), unity (*tawhid*), and justice (*adl*). Students are taught how to develop impressive personalities and contribute to a peaceful and amiable social environment through universal humanitarian virtues, such as modesty and simplicity, and through Islamic virtues, such as remaining in the state of *wudu* (ablution) and saying *Bismillah* (Quranic verse meaning *In the name of Allah*) before starting anything;this blesses the act so that things don't go wrong.

The choice of textbooks and curriculum materials infused with Islamic lessons in this way becomes the mode for some Islamic school administrations to create Islamic, civil, and modern subjectivities and to keep them compatible with each other. Unlike the traditional madrasa administrations scandalized by the government and local and foreign media for their opposition to science, computer education, and modern technology, Islamic schools take pride in teaching these subjects with an Islamic flavor.

x) Islamic School Textbooks: Creating Secular Subjectivities
During the 1980s, Zia-ul-Haq deposed Bhutto's parliamentary government to inaugurate a martial law regime that was justified by the mission to Islamize the country. Politically, this mission was in cooperation with the Reagan regime to train madrasa graduates in warfare and send them on a mission to fight the Russians in Afghanistan. Educationally, it led not only to the radicalization of madrasa education but also to the radical Islamization of curriculum in all public and private schools. Islamic studies (Islamiat) has always been taught in public and private

secular school curriculum, but in the 1980s history, social studies, and geography curriculum were transformed to represent the peoples of Pakistan in relation to Islam only. A new history was constructed in which the country's Hindu, Buddhist, and Christian political regimes, art, architecture, and legacies were scratched out. The creation of Pakistan was traced back to the day the first Muslim conqueror, Muhammad bin Qasim, set foot in Sindh (the province in which Karachi is located) and displayed heroism by demolishing all Hindu idols. Similarly, its geography was portrayed as ideal because it is surrounded by Muslim countries including Afghanistan, Iran, and indirectly Saudi Arabia. In the last decade and a half, efforts have been made to bring the country's mixed cultural traditions back to the curriculum. Islamic schools are unique in that they have embraced the concept that these mixed cultural traditions and histories are reconcilable to madrasa-style traditional Islamic theology, a factor that is often criticized by madrasa *ulama*.

Like the private secular schools, Islamic schools also have leeway in choosing their textbooks for secular subjects. This means that textbooks are different for every Islamic school and change every year. However, a recent example of a textbook series, *History in Focus,* aimed at grades 6–8, views historians as detectives and covers the Indus Valley civilization, the Aryans, the Persians, Ancient Greece and the Roman Empire, the Hindu Mauryan dynasty, the Hindu and Buddhist art and sculptural legacy in Gandhara, and the Hindu Gupta dynasty.[48] Some Islamic schools also use the *Oxford History of Pakistan Series* for grades 6 to 8, in which the first history lesson is on the evolution of man and other animals. Learning how man evolved to the *Homo erectus* stage is irreconcilable with the history of man in Islam, which begins with Adam and Eve's descent to earth.[49] However, Islamic schools are not only teaching these subjects without Islamizing the contents, but also broadening the scope of history to the stone age, Chinese philosophical thought and civilization, Western civilizations, Mesopotamian civilization, and other epochs. Similarly, the *Geography for Pakistan* series for grades 6–8 taught in Islamic schools does not locate Pakistan as part of the global Islamic community, but focuses on land formations, environment, agriculture, vegetation, and urbanization.[50]

Seventh-grader Obaid talked to me about what he likes in his history textbook. "It teaches us that there have been great and not so great rulers in every culture and that we have a lot to learn from some of the great nations. I love watching the Discovery Channel after reading about these civilizations because I can understand everything!" Another student, Asif, in sixth grade, loves his *Geography Alive* book, written by the same author who wrote the *Oxford History of Pakistan Series* because "it starts with a chapter on astronomy! . . . I want to be an astronomer when I grow up!"[51]

In this way, Islamic schools are secularizing the curricula to create a well-rounded Pakistani citizenry that is cognizant of the histories, art, philosophies, trends, and legacies that keep them competitive and informed in a global community. This includes incorporating a variety of subjects, such as evolution and the contribution of Hindus and Buddhists to Pakistan's heritage, that remind Islamic school students of the impact of other religious traditions and cultures on their culture and their country's diverse demographic.

2. Islamic School Pedagogies: Creating National Subjectivities

The Pakistani identity at Islamic schools often becomes synonymous with the Islamic identity. Using Arabic words for religious vocabulary rather than Urdu words is a linguistic marker of religiosity. As mentioned earlier, being Pakistani is equated with being Muslim. In the fifteen different Islamic schools that I visited, students were not allowed to use *Khuda hafiz*, a Persian greeting that is the traditional way of saying good-bye in Urdu. Instead, they use the Arabic word *Allah* instead of *Khuda* and say *Allah hafiz*. Such an ideology conforms to Zia-ul-Haq's Islamization and, to a large extent, is funded by Saudi Arabia to replace all Persian words in Urdu with Arabic words.

While English in private secular schools is the linguistic marker of the social practices and culture to which children are expected to adapt, at the Islamic school this marker is Arabic, signifying an alternative Islamic tradition alongside a modern, secular tradition created by the strict enforcement of English as the medium only when the students are studying science, math, and so forth.

Syed Alam, principal of the C1 school, described the school's pedagogical mission.

> What marks us as different from the West is that there, individualism is valued. In our society, as Islam teaches us, collectivism is valued. Individual praise for achievements at private secular schools creates

individualistic subjectivities in the students. They learn Islamiat to get a sense of achievement, they take interest in studies and in civil society, because it will get them somewhere. This is the root of a class culture. O-level is just a system. If we teach it our style, only then will the students not adopt the kind of culture, the kind of modernity, the kind of secular values that come with it . . . secular education is important, but so is developing collectivism, of remembering that an individual is not to be celebrated, that no individual is superior over another just because he/she knows English or has mastery over some subjects. Our society has become selfish because we celebrate ourselves . . . thank you . . . you're welcome . . . good, bad, excellent . . . celebration belongs to Allah and his prophet, peace be upon him.[52]

As Syed Alam points out, greetings and manners of speech that celebrate Allah and being a Muslim serve to create the subjectivity of a *momin* (believer) in the student and represents the class, the school assembly, and the world outside as part of a larger *ummah*. It highlights his understanding of Pakistani society as equal to the Muslim society; saving Pakistani culture is synonymous to saving an Islamic culture from Western influence. Syed Alam's comments also signify the kind of religious subjectivity created through these schools—one that does not stand in opposition to the state, as is the case in some Islamic schools in Egypt, nor in compliance to the state (see chapter 2 for a discussion on Islamic schools studied by Herrera in Cairo).[53] Instead, similar to Saba Mahmood's observation of the women's piety movement in Egypt, Pakistani Islamic schools symbolize an alternative religious tradition and provide a medium through which urban Pakistani administrators, teachers, parents, and children engage in the process of constructing multiple—religious, class, modern, and gender—subjectivities, and, as Armbrust noted, experience modernity by maintaining continuity with their religious traditions.[54] Rather, it allows for the creation of an alternative worldview to cope with the social and urban environment.

I asked an eighth grader, Danish, at C1 if he feels that the way he has learned to greet at his school is different from what his friends have learned at their schools. He replied,

I am different amongst the friends in my lane that I play cricket with and in my family. The rest of the kids in the lane say *hi* or nothing at all. Everybody instantly knows that I go to some different school when I greet in the Islamic way. Most of the people think that I must have learned it from the madrasa, but I tell them that I go to a private school. My friends' parents find me very well-behaved. My grandmother loves me when I use proper Arabic greetings.[55]

Thus, developing a reformed and informed Muslim identity within oneself is synonymous to being a good citizen of the country. In the experiences of the people interviewed, such religiosity signifies saving the institution of a joined family system and maintaining the spirit of collectivism, which are understood as strong pillars of the Pakistani culture.

3. Islamic School Pedagogies: Creating Class Subjectivities

3a) *The Importance of English*

English is the official language of Islam, a colonial legacy that holds a much higher prestige in the society than the national language, Urdu. I sat in on classes in some Islamic schools and noticed how Urdu, the national language, is used to create national subjectivities in the students, English to render prestige to the teaching, and Arabic to authenticate religious knowledge. Therefore, code-switching, the act of switching from one language to another to communicate particular social meanings, symbolizes how language represents subjectivism in the Islamic school pedagogies. Code-switching is a means of communicating particular meanings and evokes specific historical and social contexts.[56]

In the Islamic school classrooms, teachers only allow the students to speak in English, although they sometimes switch to Urdu for explanations. By using English as the medium of instruction, the Islamic schools distinguish their Islamic teaching from that of the madrasas, which use Urdu. In addition, Islamic greetings in Arabic are used frequently by the teachers, distinguishing their teaching style from that in the private secular schools. In the Islamic schools, the use of English signifies prestige, the use of Arabic signifies Islamic knowledge, and the use of Urdu signifies the national culture.

To obtain a teacher's perspective, I spoke to Ms. Shumaila at C1 about English proficiency, and she told me the following story.

One time the student drew me! I didn't know what to explain. I said, "*Jazakallah* [thanks be to Allah], but this is a human being! You were not supposed to draw humans and animals. Just things in nature." The boy stared at me blankly. I repeated the instruction in Urdu. He instantly said, "OK, miss," and drew a sunflower! So much for the administrative rule that we speak in English 100 percent of the time!

To understand how class is conceptualized and communicated in Islamic schools through English proficiency, it was also important to understand the aspiration of parents. So I spoke with Mr. Humayun, whose daughter is a seventh grader at C1, about the school's linguistic pedagogies, "We live in Federal B Area. I got her admission to this school because they are very strict about English. I want her to not just know English but also have no speaking hesitation, you know. I have also arranged for private English tutoring at home for her." I asked him in what languages he spoke to his daughter, the administration, and the teachers. He replied, "Urdu. Some of them, like the English teacher, the science teacher, reply in English half the time."[57]

Living in a lower-middle-class area and sending his child to the C1 in the middle-class area of Gulshan-e-Iqbal is an effort on the part of Mr. Humayun to create class status by allowing his child to socialize with children from other middle-class families and to become competent in using English to secure better jobs and win prestige in the society. As Mr. Humayun's comments show, choosing an English-medium Islamic school does not reflect the parent's natural linguistic choice but the kind of linguistic subjectivity he aspires to create in his child for social mobility and professional success. Mr. Humayun is clearly in awe of the English-speaking culture at C1. The tuition culture in Pakistan, for O-level subjects or private tutoring at home from underpaid college teachers, compensates for the gaps in education that first-generation, English-medium, private-school-going children cannot fill at home. For Mr. Humayun, that gap is English, which he infused in this conversation with me after every three words in Urdu to show that he knew it. From my own experience, trying to convince people in upper-class Islamic schools to talk to me, I knew that for social and professional success, that level of oral proficiency was not enough.

Now, I shall turn to presenting a contrasting experience I had speaking with the staff and the administration at C2. During my visit, I was first evaluated in my English proficiency by the administration before I could conduct interviews at the school. It was a disappointment that I was not a product of O-level education, but my private education at a school located in the most expensive area of Karachi gave me initial credibility. Still, my English was tested before the interview could begin, and when Mr. Kamran, principal at C2, found it to be sufficiently American, he asked, "What makes you live in Gulshan-e-Iqbal?" I was made to realize once more that my family residence could never match my English proficiency and that I could never succeed in being considered an upper-class citizen or worthy of navigating an elite Islamic school. So I used my best American accent and asked Mr. Kamran how they decide whether a student will succeed in gaining English proficiency even if he or she has some background in traditional Islamic education, indicating that the latter tend to be not up to the mark (read, belong to lower-class families).

Mr. Kamran got my point.

> We make sure that those cases don't make their way here. Besides, the families need to be able to afford the tuition, right? Actually, we interview parents before the students can fill out the application. If they are English-medium-school educated [private secular] and English speaking, then we enter their children on the admission waiting list. Then, we evaluate the parents' professions and where they live to judge whether the parents will continue to be capable of paying for their children's tuition. We have to maintain a particular standard . . . after all, we're not some private school in an apartment complex![58]

Schools such as the C2, which Mr. Kamran operates, have fees over Rs. 40,000 per month (US$400), which keeps from outside the Malir Cantonment area from enrolling their children. In addition, the school maintains class prestige by evaluating the parents' backgrounds in interviews. If they are affluent, they will have studied in the high-prestige convent schools or at other elite schools known for producing heads of state, politicians, and celebrities. Consider my interaction with Ms. Aania, the eighth-grade English teacher at the elite C2. When I told her about the purpose of my visit, she responded, "Very interesting research. Which block in Cantonment is your house in?"

"No, I am in the Gulshan-e-Iqbal area, actually."

She gave me a perplexed look that lasted for the rest of our conversation. I asked her about English proficiency at her school.

Ms. Aania replied in an authoritative tone. "*Nobody* speaks in Urdu here. This is not just any school in some small lane. We have standards here. The teachers here are screened for good backgrounds and then selected for the school."

I asked if all students are able to navigate in English.

Ms. Aaania answered, "There is no question of students not understanding. They are already talking in English when they come. Their parents talk in English."[59]

In the C1, students still feel at odds with English, the language they do not speak at home. The parents seek Islamic schools strict in enforcing instruction in English, but, as Mr. Humayun and Ms. Shumaila's experiences indicate, this class marker often stands artificially with the home cultural, linguistic, and cognitive frames of the students. Teachers in the middle-income area Islamic schools, such as Ms. Shumaila, negotiate these class, linguistic, and religious subjectivities on a daily basis. In contrast to this, Mr. Kamran gentrifies the school by gentrifying the school at the pre-enrollment stage—by guaranteeing that only students from affluent, English-speaking families are considered. The fact that C2 is located in the elite Malir Cantonment area guarantees this gentrification.

Mr. Saqib, in charge of admissions at C1, spoke to me about the school's rule on English speaking.

> You must understand that we are all trying to do our level best. High-proficiency-level English teachers demand a very high salary. We don't have the kind of infrastructure to hire them. But we have a very congenial atmosphere in the school and I try to push the teachers to keep an English-speaking atmosphere only. Some senior [female] teachers do it more naturally. Others are trying . . . we have added another activity . . . an extra half hour everyday of English conversation . . . students who go back to Urdu lose marks and their parents are sent warning letters about their behavior. That way, parents are satisfied and they know clearly when it is their child's fault.[60]

Private Islamic schooling is a class statement. While Mr. Kamran and Ms. Aania's perspectives highlight how people's access to Islamic education is gentrified by class, Mr. Humayun, Ms. Shumaila and Mr. Saqib's perspectives highlight that the contenders' (administration, teachers, parents, and students) often struggle with social and familial norms to actively construct that prestigious religious educational environment. Thus, Islamic schools are not simply places to seek religious education. Rather, they are a vehicle to maintain and transform class, with language as a symbolic capital, and professional subjectivities.

4. Creating Gender Subjectivities

Teachers as Nurturers

Traditionally, in Pakistan teaching has long been a profession associated with women, especially at the primary, secondary, and intermediate/high school levels. Between 95 to 98 percent of the teaching staff at Islamic schools is female. The administration in Islamic schools is very sensitive to their conflation with the madrasas, where, except for the full-fledged female adult madrasas, students of ages four to thirteen are taught by males. Islamic school administrators are sensitive to the fact that male priests are associated with the brainwashing and the maltreatment of the students in these madrasas. As a result, whatever the educational, ideological, class, political, and ethnolinguistic backgrounds of the Islamic school patrons, the schools unanimously prefer to keep female teachers and staff over males. I asked administrators at nine different Islamic schools about the gender ratio of their teaching and administrative staff. At all these schools, the principals informed me that female employees are preferred, though exceptions are made in the areas of computer education and accounting, fields in which women interested in teaching seldom pursue degrees. The principal of an Islamic school located in Clifton, an upper-middle- to upper-class area of Karachi, informed me, "Women teachers are like mothers. They understand the value of nurturing in education, they know when to beat and how much to beat for punishment. Men are rash with children, lose control over their anger and cannot differentiate petty from major misconduct."[61] The head of the administration at another Islamic school, located in a middle-class area, North Nazimabad, described his school's preference for female teachers in this way, "Female teachers do not take days off and do not resort to physical punishment in anger like male teachers do."[62]

Mr. Rehman, vice principal at the C2 spoke to me about why he prefers to hire female teachers.

> I employed a male madrasa graduate, a *hafiz-e-Quran*, who had nine years' experience conducting *hifz* classes. Not even a month had passed when I began getting complaints from parents about harsh language and threat of physical punishment. From then onwards, I decided that men are just not cut out for the kind of soft teaching that we want at this school.[63]

I asked Asad, a ninth grader, how he liked his *hifz* teacher, "The *hifz* ma'am doesn't smile much." I asked him if she punished, too. "She gives penance sometimes or calls the parents if we do not show progress in *nazira* and *hifz*. She never beats anyone [though]," he said.[64] The social and educational backgrounds and pay scales of the *alimat* teaching *hifz* and *nazira* classes at Islamic schools are no different than those of madrasa teachers. Yet the administrations are willing to work with them because, as Mr. Hakeem, the vice principal of an Islamic school located in Malir, a working- to lower-middle-class area of Karachi, confided, "We do not want to be equated with the madrasas."[65] Mr. Hakeem elaborated on the popular discourse about the madrasas that the administration and faculty there physically and sexually abuse the students. The discourse emerges from the fact that madrasas appeal to the poor: mothers leave children at the madrasas from morning until evening or for permanent boarding, in which case madrasas serve as boarding schools. Thus, with no accountability, illiterate families, desperate for shelter and food, have no recourse when their children receive severe punishments. This manhandling associated with the madrasas has led to the perception that religious schooling is abusing children under the façade of religious instruction. The Islamic schools are very sensitive to this charge. In the fifteen Islamic schools I visited in Karachi, strict measures are taken against any staff person dispensing anything harsher than what are regarded as regular punishments in public and private schools of Pakistan—telling children to stand outside the class or to stay after school, scolding, canceling breaks, and so forth.[66] Mr. Mukhtar, an administrator at an Islamic school in the working-class area of Lyari, commented on the disadvantages of keeping male teachers: "They are egoistic and you try to stop them from following their way, and next time they will take revenge on the student by giving more severe punishment."[67] Islamic school administrators like Mr. Mukhtar, therefore, prefer female staff, not only because they execute less harsh punishments, but also because when they do, the administration believes that it can advise them otherwise.

Increasing Women's Role in the Public Sphere

Unlike the madrasas, Islamic schools provide proper computer lab services to their secondary students. Computer education textbook covers show girls with scarfs operating computers and promote women's right to become computer literate and professionally promising alongside men in the public sphere. This ideology stands in contrast to orthodox madrasas' discourse that women's computer education is un-Islamic and goes against their gender role of homemakers. Computer literacy also highlights the middle and upper-class urban parents' ideology of seeing their daughters as educated professionals and mothers. Any fear of computer education diverting girls from their primary role of representing their family's chastity in the public domain is prevented by the girls' Islamic dress code.[68]

Ms. Sadia, the Urdu teacher at C2, spoke to me about what working at an Islamic school means for her.

> When I was in intermediate [high school], there was a lot of pressure on me from my family to end my education there. They would say that you'd be married off soon and thereafter you'd get busy taking care of the household and bringing up children. I thought that I was done with education. Then the proposals didn't look suitable, and so I began and finished my BA . . . I have a sister older than me and she must get married first . . . so, just for *time pass* . . . I convinced my parents to let me work here . . . the environment was moral and the institute is to convey Islamic knowledge . . . once I started working here, I realized how much experience others have and there are so many women teachers who are pursuing a higher degree in Islamic education or doing MA Private [an MA program affiliated with the university system for which candidates can do self-study at home and using university libraries and appear in the nationwide private MA exams]. So, I recently got enrolled for an MA, too![69]

For Ms. Sadia, working at an Islamic school has been a liberating experience. She would not have chosen to work had it not been for a place with an Islamic environment, implying gender segregation and veiling, and it became her outlet to participate in the public domain. The experience is liberating, because she no longer feels that getting married, as she was told in high school, is her only purpose in life. Instead, the Islamic school environment is proving to be an avenue for more intellectual growth; as an MA Private candidate, Ms. Sadia does not need to attend a co-gendered public university and can still look forward to more education and a salary increase at work. It is important to see the popularity of Islamic schools versus madrasas and private secular schools as mediums for teachers to break away from the social expectation of prioritizing marriage, family, and motherhood against education and career.

To examine the student perspective on the issue, I spoke to Saira, a ninth grader at C2 during recess (snack break) who spoke on why female teachers are important at her school. "My aunt quotes that a child's education starts from home," she said. "A woman's job is twofold. To have enough Islamic education to pass on good morals and to possess the education that helps her run the household in a sophisticated manner."[70]

It is important to think of this narrative in relation to that of a parent. Mr. Imran, whose son is a fifth grader at C2, had this to say about the role of women teachers at Islamic schools:

> A teacher is a child's second mother. It is tradition for a child to learn quls [last four Quranic chapters starting with the word *Say*] and *kalimas* from his/her mother. A child follows the mom the most. It is therefore important to have a lady teacher in school. Kids consider them like their moms and learn amidst the love and soft image of it. A male teacher can intimidate a child from coming to school.[71]

During fieldwork, I met a diverse group of female teachers who told me about how this incentive encouraged them to become workers and to what extent Islamic schools open the door to their professional development. At another Jamaat-e-Islami–operated Islamic school in the middle-class neighborhood of Gulshan-e-Iqbal, I asked Ms. Hira, the seventh-grade math teacher if she chose the school because she could not find a job at a private secular school. "No," she replied.

> When it was time to choose between science and arts at the high school and Bachelor's levels, I was only in love with math and wanted to do pre-engineering. My family insisted that it was no use, as I wouldn't really be able to use it in my family life. I told them that because I was never going to be a career woman, it didn't matter what I chose to study, so I might as well choose something I knew I could do well! After [bachelor's] graduation, I just stayed at home. Then I saw that this Islamic type of school had opened up in my neighborhood, and I asked my family if I could apply for a teaching job here. They figured

it was safe, there were no males in the faculty, and that it would be the right thing to do.

She paused and remained silent for a few minutes. I broke the tension by recognizing her math abilities and my fear of the subject. She suddenly came closer and said, "I hope you'll not relate the interview to the principal . . . see, they employed me for math, and now I have to teach general science for two other grades as well for the same salary. It's been two years, and they haven't revised the salary once!" She suddenly stepped back, as if realizing that she'd shared too much. She then gave me a comforting smile and said, "But it's better than wasting time at home!"[72]

Compared to the previous generation, the number of women receiving Bachelor's and Master's degrees has risen drastically in places like Karachi. Although a substantial percentage of women receive Bachelor's and Master's degrees, most never enter the job market because families consider it inappropriate for women to work and the image of a working woman is often one of immorality and greed. By contrast, women like Ms. Hira, who teaches children at an Islamic school, can justify working by considering it an act in the service of Islam and an avenue for experiencing the traditional role of woman, that is, of a mother.

Since Islamic schools are private, the government does not regulate teachers' salaries. Compared to men, who provide for their own and often their extended families, female teachers are preferred at Islamic schools because they are ready to work at a minimal salary, a factor that has nevertheless substantially contributed to the increase of middle-class, educated women in the work sector. Consider the statistical analysis below on the differences between teachers in private and public schools.[73]

A. Private schools hire 76 percent female teachers, compared to public schools, which hire 43 percent.
B. Private school teachers are substantially younger, with an average age of twenty-five years, compared to teachers in public schools, where the average age is thirty-eight years.
C. Teachers at private schools are less likely to be married (77% are single) versus 15% at public schools.
D. Only 4% of private school teachers have Master's degrees compared to 19% of teachers at public schools.

E. Only 6% of private school teachers have ever received any educational training, compared to 71% at public schools.

The private schools, including the Islamic schools that I visited, generally pay low salaries to their staff, and even lower to female staff.

An average female teacher in a government school earns Rs. 5,897 [approximately US$59] per month, which is not very different from the earnings for an average male (Rs. 6,408) [approximately US$65]. Among private schools, though, male teachers earn merely Rs. 1,789 [approximately US$18] per month, while females earn just Rs. 1,069 [approximately US$11].[74]

Gender disparity in private school salaries may not be as relevant as much as low salaries in general and the fact that teachers end up doing administrative duties and teaching many more classes than they were originally hired for. Teachers, therefore, seek private schools in upper-class areas to receive better salaries. The female teachers and staff that I met at various Islamic schools were young women who earned low wages, especially in comparison to the few male staff who largely worked in supervisory and administrative capacities. Other teachers, such as Ms. Mehnaz, complained that she did not receive her monthly paychecks regularly, was frequently called over weekends to cover more workload while the school was closed, and received no benefits or job security because of working in a private school.[75]

Until recently, graduates from madrasas (see educational levels in chapter 3) taught in madrasas or provided religious instruction in middle- and upper-class households. With the emergence of Islamic schools, now *alimat* are seeking jobs as Islamiat, *hifz* and *nazira* teachers. Islamic school administrators' tend to prefer female teachers. The ulema and alimat generally come from orthodox families. Teachers for English, math, science, social studies, and other subjects may be orthodox, liberals, may not practice Islam, or may profess other faiths, in particular, Christianity. An interesting phenomenon in Islamic schools is the mix of faculty from traditional religious institutions and from secular institutions, unprecedented in private education. Ms. Tehmina, a Montessori directress at an Islamic school located in the upper middle-class neighborhood of PECHS in Karachi, elaborated: "The administration interviews graduates from Pakistani madrasas only, but on a merit basis. The interview comprises of cross-questioning and knowledge testing, after which you are employed as assistant teachers and teachers."[76]

Sitting at an Islamic school in the middle-class area of North Nazimabad, I asked a group of four teachers, one of them being an *alima* (female Islamic scholar) about their educational and family backgrounds. The *alima* was quiet, and the rest of the women exchanged looks. Then the *alima* spoke,

> Of course if we are teaching in an Islamic school, we come from families that share our outlook in life. Others in my family may not have acquired any degree in religion but that is because making provisions for everyday problems didn't allow them to. In my family, I am a trainer of my younger brothers and sisters and they will, *inshallah*, acquire professional success in both religious and earthly worlds.

Everyone sat quietly. The *alima* felt the tension and left.

I repeated the question to a remaining teacher. She looked out to make sure that the *alima* wasn't at the door. It is common for the administrators in private schools to use teachers for spying, to ensure that the teachers are not chatting away in their free time. In Islamic schools, I gathered after a few visits that the spying was even more important to ensure that the diverse teaching staff strictly adhered to the moral code of the school. The teacher then said, "Nobody in my house is the way I am. Even I went to a secular school, college and university. I am just teaching here because—" Another teacher interrupted in excitement, "She's engaged and she'll quit two weeks before October 14, her wedding day!" I asked if others had similar plans. The teacher for Islamiat said that she had already had her *nikah* (wedding) and was waiting for her visa papers to arrive from the United Kingdom to go live with her husband. "I do not want to suffocate at home in my mother-in-law's company. That's why I am teaching here."[77] I asked the third teacher, in charge of the Montessori training, Ms. Natasha, what her family life was like, and she told me that she was single.

> My family cannot understand why I am doing this. Here, the principal and people in the administration tell us that we should govern every aspect of our life the Islamic way. My family is very modern. My brother makes designs for Aamir Adnan's shirts [a popular and

prestigious men's brand] in Pakistan and my brother's name is taken off and sold at the stores. I wonder whether it is right to do what he does. He told me that as long as you do it with good conscience, no profession is bad. My friends and family tell me how much I have transformed ever since I started working here. I don't want to be a hypocrite. If I wear an abaya and then take it off after school, it's cheating. My family calls me mullani [female mullah]!"

I asked her what her sisters were like. "I have one. She's normal. I mean, neither like me [the teacher was dressed in a burqa/cloak] nor like *out* [wild], you know." I next asked her what made her choose that school.

When you do the Montessori training course, the institute finds temporary employment for you. You do an internship with some school where they arrange your employment for a year or more, and then, if you want, you can switch. So I was sent to this school. I will finish my one year in two months from now. That doesn't mean that I will abandon this school. But I don't know. They don't pay so well, you know, and we have demanded better salary so many times.

Others looked up and nodded.[78]

Islamic schools find well-qualified and less demanding teachers in women. However, the fact that the administration does not pay them equal to the workload largely attracts middle- and upper-class women looking for a pastime in teaching, because it is the most socially acceptable career choice before they get married. Islamic schools thus prefer employing female teachers, as Mr. Hakeem, vice principal of an Islamic school in Malir, Karachi, described above, but are constantly posting job advertisements because female staff do not stay in one job for long due to marital and familial demands.

Islamic school entrepreneurs endorse three ideologies through their staffing choices: That women can work if they abide by the traditional norms of Islamic appearance, modesty, and practice; that by putting students under the supervision of women teachers, Islamic schools are putting them in nurturing hands, a discourse based on the assumption that women cannot promote militant extremism in the students like male madrasa teachers; and that, unlike the gender role promoted by the madrasas that women must stay at home, the Islamic schools want women with BA and MA degrees from secular and Islamic universities to teach in a co-educational environment. In this way, Islamic schools promote the agenda of feminist and women's rights organizations in the country, by using a modern interpretation of Islam.

In a country where a male child is preferred over a female child, strained budgets make parents choose quality, private education for boys and public education for their girls. Since the majority of Islamic schools charge less than private secular schools, especially those opened by madrasa alumni and are attached to their religious endowment, Islamic schools have not only created a workspace for educated females but have also encouraged parents to send girls to private schools.

Consider the experience of Zahra, mother of three girls and a boy who lives in a joined family house in the lower-middle-class neighborhood of Federal B Area in Karachi. She told me that her daughters had gone to a public school and the boy, the youngest, had been sent to a private secular school, because the husband wanted the son to do O-levels.

> It was difficult to wait on the girls' school bus and go pick up the boy. Then he [the husband] found out about this Islamic school. They gave us a good tuition package for the girls, and the environment is safe. They have a separate building for boys. So we got a tuition deal for four kids for less than what they charge for three kids.[79]

Zehra's is one of the many households with a limited budget in which male children are preferred for access to quality private schooling, since they are expected to run the family when they grow up, whereas girls live with their husbands' families. Commercial Islamic schools provide not only a good tuition package for Zehra's children, but also convince her husband of private schooling because of the moral environment for O-level education that will also prepare his girls for their future gender roles. It is interesting to note how the word *safe* is used to symbolize the kind of Western modernity that some Islamic school patrons attach to education in private secular schools, along with the mixed-gender environment. The fact that the parents chose public schooling for their girls in the first place points to the fact that they did prioritize a well-rounded modern education for the girls that was virtually free, as opposed to sending them to a free madrasa. Thus, for girls from such families, Islamic school education creates an alternative gender and educational experience; it allows them to seek privileged education and be equal to the boys. Later, as some Islamic schoolteachers do, the girls can obtain a Montessori directress certificate to teach at any private school and earn an income.

To understand the student perspective on the issue, I asked Zehra's daughter, eighth-grader Faiza, how she found the shift from a private secular school to an Islamic school. She said, "I used to have a lot of friends in my previous school. I miss them, and I don't like that there're more [Islamic] subjects here as part of the curriculum. Other students started them from first grade and I have joined only now, so everyone else is way ahead of me." I asked her what she liked about the education at the Islamic school.

> The emphasis on English. In the public school, there was no English outside the classroom. And I like the computer classes here. I use the school computer three to four times a week. I use Facebook, Twitter in the computer class. For all this and so many other things, you need English. So I like how they stress using it all the time here. I ask my computer sir a lot of questions. I was happy at my previous school, but people didn't notice my school first. Now they notice, they ask me to describe my private school to them. I feel good when I tell people which school I go to; it's Islamic and it's private. I can make friends with a lot of girls in my lane, my family friends, and my relatives who are doing O-levels, which I will soon begin preparing for [in ninth grade]. I have added over fifty friends on Facebook in the last few weeks. They are from Islamic schools in Defense, Malir Cantonment, and . . . those areas. So I feel . . . valued.

I asked if her online friends' community included boys. "Yes, sure. If they are from an Islamic school, I do, because the boys from Islamic schools are very well mannered."[80] Growing up in a lower-middle-income area, Faiza seemed to be sensitive about her class. Through Islamic schools, she has acquired class as well as respect as a girl who goes to an Islamic school. Rather than being cast as a poor and passive student of a madrasa, she is now regarded as an English-speaking, modern girl who, because of her association with the Islamic school system, is regarded as worthy of friendship by the elite Islamic school-goers on the Internet. Computer education at Islamic schools has allowed her to transcend her father's moral rules and define a *safe* social environment on her own in the mix-gendered online community, as well as to overcome the economic limitation of not having access to a computer at home. Through Islamic schools, she has entered the community that until now only her brother was a part of—that of private school-goers.

Conclusion

Schooling is an arena where aspirations, pedagogical implementation, experiences, and curriculum interact with diverse student groups to produce varying subjectivities.[81] In this chapter, I described how Islamic schools cater to the varied needs of Karachiites and how the schools function to create class, sectarian, ethnic, communal, and political subjectivities in the students simultaneously. Particular to the Islamic school pedagogies is how Islam is reconciled with secular modernity by varying uses of Arabic with English and by Islamizing secular learning with specially designed textbooks. Islamic schools creatively carve out alternative social, religious, and political spaces in Karachi. The manners of imparting secular knowledge, of teaching greeting and conduct, of conducting morning assembly, of combining cognition with Islamic education, and of making Islamic education compatible with status concerns, sectarian traditions, gender norms, and civil values distinguish Islamic schools from madrasas and private secular schools and identify them as trendsetters in Western-style modern and Islamic traditional education.

CHAPTER 6

Toward a New Approach to Islamic Education

The production of soldiers by Pakistani madrasas during the Cold War and their recent association with terrorist attacks in the United States and the United Kingdom ignited a lot of interest in understanding the psyche of Muslims and their views on Islamic education. However, this exploration focused on Muslim extremists and madrasas as their breeding grounds. Such an approach assumes that the message from all formal institutions of Islamic education is homogeneous and that their students are passive receivers of knowledge. Whereas in Pakistan, it is common knowledge that madrasas cater to the poor, living in slums, and are not the primary educational choice for those who can afford to pay for education; studies have not prioritized understanding the mainstream Muslim citizens from the middle and upper classes, their educational choices, or the ways in which they make Islam, to use Starrett's term, *functional* to their socioeconomic needs and political and ideological concerns.[1]

By highlighting the reasons for the recent patronization of a modern Islamic schooling trend in Pakistan, my aim was to draw attention to what moderate urban citizens are saying to the state and to the international world about their relationship with Islamic tradition in their educational and social lives. My class observations and interviews with administrators, teachers, parents, and students bring attention to the fact that students of religion are not just passive receivers of a monolithic tradition. Rather, class and status needs and sectarian, gender, political, and ethnic aspirations of the consumers and producers of these schools inform and interact with the pedagogical process to create various kinds of subjectivities in the students. By presenting data on how Islamic schools' assembly routines, classroom practices, and in-school activities create subjectivities in teachers, students, and parents, I have argued for a more nuanced, critical, versified, and complex approach to understanding the subjectivities created through Islamic education. I have also stressed through my observations that the religious and social subjectivities of students from these schools are completely different from those of students attending madrasas, public, and private secular schools.

As evidenced in my observations and conversations with teachers, administrators, students, and parents, the private Islamic schooling educational experiment does not simplistically create religious subjectivities in the students. Islamic school students do not reside in the schools, as is the case in madrasas. They are not involved in missionary activities at school, in mosques, and at religious congregations that turn students and teachers at madrasas into an isolated community with no critical engagement with the professional, educational, and social concerns in the larger society. The schools' students, administration, and teachers continue to live diverse social, family, and professional lives, and satisfy their ideological, political, communal, professional, and social prestige concerns through active engagement and participation in this new educational medium. They critique the notion that religious schooling only creates religious subjectivities and that students experience religious education passively and in social isolation. Rather, as Paul Willis argued, the Karachi urbanites deliberately seek to construct certain religious and class subjectivities in their children that complement their sectarian, class, and ethnic interests.[2] Instead of revealing Islamic school students as passive victims of brainwashing, my interviews with the students underscored how every student identifies with, absorbs, denies, and promotes the schools' particular religious ideology and class interests through his/her own critical engagement.

In Chapter 5, by drawing attention to how the gentrification of the school clientele based on social class makes the environment and pedagogy at each Islamic school different from the other, I argue for a rejection of abstract accounts of Islamic education constructed in isolation from the socioeconomic concerns of the community. As I highlight in Chapter 4, Islamic school patrons are reviving Islamic tradition, but only after ensuring that it is in accordance with sectarian, subsectarian, political, and ethnic concerns. Not only that, but the schools also ensure social prestige through British education and a chance at upward social mobility to the students when they choose Islamic schools in upper-class areas.

Discussing agency, Talal Asad notes, "People are never only active agents and subjects in their own history. The interesting question in each case is: In what degree and in what way are they agents or patients?"[3] The patronization of private Islamic schooling by middle- and upper-class urbanites demonstrates how Pakistanis are not simply choosing Islamic schooling for their children because they are religious institutions. Rather, the failure of the state to provide quality public education and the radicalization of traditional madrasa education under Zia-ul-Haq during the Cold War era led to a quiet revolution on the part of moderate citizens to move toward private secular schools. True, anyone looking at post-1980s-Islamization Pakistan, the growing dominance of the Saudi Wahhabi (Saudi orthodox) sect, and the recent history of Shiite-Sunni conflicts in Karachi is bound to read the patronization of Islamic schools as a sign of the Islamization of the society post-Zia regime. However as I sat in on Islamic school classes and spoke to teachers, parents, administrators, and the students, it became hard for me to reduce the agencies of these people to the passive adaptation of the Islamization and a one-dimensional radicalization of the society. The popularity of Islamic schools points to the failure of the state to provide a unified system of public education or to define the role of Islam and English language in the white-collar job market that has led middle- and upper-class citizens to rely on expensive private schools. Where the Musharraf government's crackdown on madrasas in 2002 brought much support from middle- and upper-class citizens, it also made them acutely aware of the international mockery it made of traditional Islamic learning. Parochial schools seem to be meeting a need of urban Pakistanis growing up under Zia's Islamization to find a balance between state-imposed Islam, Communism, and Islamic extremism that also allows for the privileges of private secular schools to continue.

Recent anthropological literature has highlighted the relation between Islamic practice and class concerns. Through the Islamic school example, I urge that this relationship also be explored in the educational sphere. Concerns such as securing white-collar jobs in the highly competitive market of Karachi and ensuring class elevation encourage middle-class families to seek Montessori education at the pre-primary level and foreign English-medium education at the primary and secondary levels. While parochial school patrons care for the prestige associated with O-level education at private secular schools, they also note that the government Islamiat syllabus does not train students in the traditional religious education of *hifz*, *nazira*, and *hadith*, and that madrasas are not providing these with critical thinking. As I highlighted in chapter 5, through language use, textbooks, and pedagogical styles, parochial schools are providing a modern and balanced blend of Western education, Pakistani culture, and Islamic traditions to families.

My interviews and observations demonstrate that for the administrators, teachers, and patrons, such schools are an effort to define Islam as modern and to reconstruct traditional Islamic education as a domain in which Western-style secular, modern education that caters to class and professional elevation can co-exist with religious tradition. Borrowing Herrera's argument that Western, colonial, secular education is not passively adopted by the people nor does such education describe their experiences of modernity, I drew attention to the fact that the Islamic school staff, students, and parents understand the secular in Western O-level education as an instrument for worldly success and social prestige rather than a way of life.[4] Many of my informants saw the colonial O-level educational model as having Westernized private schools so much that children were deviating from their own cultural and religious values. Still, others who previously aspired to send children to prestigious private secular schools informed me that their choice of private Islamic education was guided by the fact that their children could break away from socially immoral and/or un-Islamic habits, described as variedly as using drugs, lavish spending, and Western dressing, greeting, and social networking styles. The parents' choice of Islamic schools thus shows their agency in integrating the modern, secular, colonial model of education with Islamic and Pakistani values. In this way, to echo Armbrust's argument, unlike the Western experience of modernity, Pakistani urbanites are experiencing modernity by maintaining continuity with their religious tradition.[5]

My fieldwork is the first attempt at a systematic study of the private Islamic schooling phenomenon in Pakistan. Given my focus on the diversity of communities the schools cater to in Karachi alone, this study is not exhaustive and provides only a bird's eye view of this otherwise burgeoning phenomenon in the country's urban centers. Using the cultural and urban landscape of Pakistan as a point of departure, I have noted in chapter 2 that, while the historical, political, cultural, economic, and urban conditions that have led to the proliferation of these schools in Pakistan are particular to the country and its urban populace, the parochial Islamic schooling trend is fast gaining currency in other Muslim communities in Asia and the Middle East. Though efforts began in the early 1990s, the post-9/11 politics, the stigma that practicing Muslims are conservative and resistant to change, and the need to find a feasible solution to quality public education and to reconcile and standardize madrasa education have catalyzed these reform initiatives.

More ethnographic and historical accounts are needed to understand this global parochial educational experiment, but that first requires that such experiments are not looped in the same category as madrasas, as much as there is a need to define the latter more diversely. It also requires a closer examination of the historical, political, national, class, economic, professional, sectarian, and communal conditions and concerns that guide people's choice to patronize a particular brand of Islamic education. The choice of schooling in turn determines the meanings of Islamic tradition, modernity, and secularism and the subjectivities created through the schooling process.

Finally, the case of Pakistan shows that Islamic schools are being patronized by middle- and upper-class citizens. For some, they are a class symbol, and for others a new configuration of the golden period of Islamic theological tradition, when it was informed by Quran and *hadith*, but in ways that legitimize the need to mold it to modern and secular concerns in an urban present. Madrasa education, except for a large amount of information for a limited period, is considered low-esteem in the middle- and upper-classes and is largely associated with the poor, who need the free food and lodging. To understand alternative formal Islamic educational traditions, therefore, the producers, patrons, and receivers of knowledge need to be differentiated along more than religious lines and as active agents in functionalizing Islam and using it as a conduit for the creation and projection of an enlightened and critical local and global citizenry.

Notes

Chapter 1

1. Interview, July 13, 2005, Sunni madrasa, Gulshan-e-Iqbal, Karachi.
2. Srinivas, *The Remembered Village*.
3. Interview, July 25, 2007, Islamic school, Gulshan-e-Iqbal, Karachi.
4. Altorki and El-Solh, eds. *Arab Women in the Field*.
5. Interview, August 17, 2007, Shiite Islamic school, Rizvia Society, Karachi.
6. Interview, August 21, 2007, Shiite Islamic school, Rizvia Society, Karachi.
7. Riaz, Volume I, July 2007.
8. Candland, *Pakistan's Recent Experience*, 160.

Chapter 2

1. Dhofier, *The Pesantren Tradition*.
2. Ibid.
3. Liow, Joseph Chinyong. *The Challenge of Islamic Reformism*.
4. Hefner and Zaman (Eds.), *Schooling Islam*, p. 2.
5. Herrera, *Sanctity of the School*.
6. Ibid., 168.
7. Ibid., 109.
8. Ibid.
9. Interview, October 19, 2007, Islamic school, Gulshan-e-Iqbal, Karachi.
10. Ibid.
11. Sikand, *Bastions of the Believers*.
12. Interview, July 27, 2007, the late Mr. Khusro's residence, Gulshan-e-Iqbal, Karachi.
13. Sikand, *Bastions of the Believers*.
14. Malik, *Madrasas in South Asia*.
15. Yoginder Sikand, *Bastions of the Believers*.

16. Ambikar, *Embodying the Enemy*.
17. Survey-based interviews, August–December 2007, Islamic schools in Gulshan-e-Iqbal, PECHS, Defense, Gulistan-e-Jauhar, Clifton, Karachi.
18. Riaz, volume III.
19. Interview, Shiite Islamic school, April 2, 2008, Lyari, Karachi.
20. Hefner and Zaman, *Schooling Islam*.
21. Interview, July 14, 2004, bookstore, Park Towers, Clifton, Karachi.
22. Asad, *Anthropology of Islam*, 14.
23. Haj, *Reconfiguring Islamic Tradition*.
24. Riaz, volumes I–III.
25. Interview, October 2, 2007, Islamic school, North Nazimabad, Karachi.
26. Esposito, *Unholy War*.
27. Interview, September 17, 2007, Islamic school, Nazimabad, Karachi.
28. Ouis, *Power, Person, and Place*, 332.
29. Giroux, *Theory and Resistance in Education*, 42–71.
30. Said, *Orientalism*.
31. Nawaz, *Islam and Muslim Psyche*.
32. Sivan, *Radical Islam*; Kepel, *Jihad*; Stern, *Terror*.
33. Riaz, volume I.
34. Haj, *Reconfiguring Islamic Tradition*.
35. Ibid., 1.
36. Malik, *Colonialization of Islam*.
37. Anzar, *Islamic Education*; Hoodbhoy, *Education and the State*; Looney, *Reforming Pakistan's Educational System*.
38. Riaz, volume I.
39. Eickelman, *Mass Higher Education*, 643.
40. Interview, September 20, 2007, Islamic school, PECHS, Karachi.
41. Asad, *Anthropology of Islam*; Masud, *Communicative Action*.
42. Roy, *Secularism Confronts Islam*.
43. Ibid., 67.
44. Ibid.
45. Wafaqul Madaris, 22.
46. Wafaqul Madaris, May 2007, 34.
47. Roy, *Secularism Confronts Islam*, 67.
48. Armbrust, *Mass Culture*.
49. Hirschkind, *Passional Preaching*, 537.
50. Mahmood, *Politics of Piety*, 5, 6.
51. Ibid., 6.
52. Ibid., 6.
53. Ibid.
54. Interview, September 3, 2007, Sunni Islamic school, Bahadurabad, Karachi.

55. Ibid.
56. Jones, *Pakistan: Eye of the Storm*; Abbas, *Pakistan's Drift into Extremism*; Stern, *Terror*; Kaplan, *Soldiers of God*; Ali, *The Duel*.
57. Hoodbhoy, *Education and the State*; International Crisis Group, *Pakistan: Madrassas*; International Crisis Group, *Pakistan: The Mullah and the Military*; Hussain, *Study of Jamia Ashrafia*; Government of Pakistan, *Deeni Madaris ki Jame Report [Urdu]*; Government of Pakistan, *National Education Policy;* Government of Pakistan, *National Education Policy*.
58. Popkewitz and Fendler, eds., *Critical Theories in Education;* Reed-Danahay, *Education and Identity;* Dixson and Rousseau, *Critical Race Theory in Education;* Willis, *Learning to Labor*; Apple, *Teachers and Texts*.
59. Starrett, *Putting Islam to Work*.
60. Ibid., 2.
61. Riaz, volume II, survey, November 10–24, 2008, Islamic schools in Gulistan-e-Jauhar, Defense and Federal B Area.
62. Zeghal, *Religion and Politics in Egypt*.
63. Levinson, *The Place of Educational Discourse,* 598.
64. Ibid., 599.
65. Willis, *Learning to Labor*; Spindler, *Education and Cultural Process*; Dance, *Tough Fronts*; Anderson-Levitt, *Local Meanings, Global Schooling*; Ostrove and Cole, *Privileging Class*.
66. Ogbu, *The Next Generation*.
67. Willis, *Learning to Labor*.
68. Interviews, Sept–November 2007, Islamic schools in Defense, Malir Cantonment, and Clifton.
69. Interview, January 25, 2008, Islamic school, Defense, Karachi.
70. Giroux, *Theory and Resistance in Education*.
71. Herrera, *Education, Islam, and Modernity*.
72. MacLeod, *Accommodating Protest*.
73. Herrera, *The Sanctity of the School*.
74. Interview, July 23, 2007, Karachi.
75. Bourdieu, *Distinction*.
76. Ibid., 114.
77. Survey-based interviews, September 1–29, 2007, Islamic schools in Gulshan-e-Iqbal, Gulistan-e-Jauhar, North Nazimabad, and F. B. Area.
78. Bengelsdorf, Cerullo, and Yogesh Chandrani, eds., *Selected Writings of Eqbal Ahmad*.
79. Interview, September 14, 2007, Jamaat-e-Islami Islamic school, Gulshan-e-Iqbal, Karachi.
80. Interview, December 20, 2007, Karachi.

Chapter 3

1. Hoodbhoy, *Education and the State*.
2. Ibid.
3. Ibid.
4. Human Rights Commission of Pakistan, 2004.
5. Hoodbhoy, *Education and the State*.
6. Abbas, *The Power of English*.
7. Government of Pakistan, *National Education Policy 1998–2010*.
8. Ibid.
9. Hoodbhoy, *Education and the State*, 215–250.
10. Hoodbhoy, *Education and the State*.
11. Ibid.
12. Interview, February 3, 2008, Shiite madrasa, Rizvia Society, Karachi.
13. Qadeer, *Pakistan*.
14. Hoodbhoy, *Education and the State*.
15. Tambiah, *Leveling Crowds*.
16. Rahman, *Denizens of Alien Worlds*.
17. Hoodbhoy, *Education and the State*.
18. Ochs, *Clarification and Culture*.
19. Rahman, *Denizens of Alien Worlds*.
20. Haqqani, *The Role of Islam*.
21. Interview, August 21, 2007, Sunni madrasa, PECHS, Karachi.
22. Hoodbhoy, *Education and the State*.
23. Government of Pakistan, *National Education Policy*, 1979.
24. Jaffrelot, *A History of Pakistan*.
25. Hoodbhoy, *Education and the State*.
26. Government of Pakistan, *National Education Policy 1992–2002*.
27. Ibid.
28. Ibid; Lodhi, *Mosque-schools*.
29. Hoodbhoy, *Education and the State*.
30. Abbas, *The Power of English*.
31. Raza, *Zulfikar Ali Bhutto and Pakistan*.
32. Khan, *Basic Education in Rural Pakistan*.
33. Hoodbhoy, *Education and the State*.
34. Rahman, *Language, Religion and Identity*.
35. Hoodbhoy, *Education and the State*.
36. Government of Pakistan, *National Education Policy 1998–2010*.
37. Rahman, *Language, Religion and Identity*.
38. Hoodbhoy, *Education and the State*.
39. Government of Pakistan, *National Education Policy*, 1959.

40. Constitution of the Islamic Republic of Pakistan, Article 251, 1973.
41. Rahman, *Denizens of Alien Worlds*; Government of Pakistan, *National Education Policy*, 1979.
42. Hoodbhoy, *Education and the State*.
43. Interview, January 12, 2008, Islamic school, Gulshan-e-Iqbal, Karachi.
44. Cohen, *The Idea of Pakistan*.
45. Ibid.
46. Ali, *The Duel*.
47. Ibid.
48. Ibid.
49. Ibid.
50. Malik, *Madrasas in South Asia*.
51. Ibid.
52. Ibid.
53. Ali, *The Duel;* Malik, *Madrasas in South Asia*.
54. Ibid.
55. Malik, *Madrasas in South Asia*.
56. Ali, *The Duel*.
57. Interviews on August 3, August 27, and September 5, 2007, at three madrasas, Karachi.
58. Interview, September 16, 2007, Sunni madrasa, Gulshan-e-Iqbal, Karachi.
59. Interview, January 23, 2008, *The Guidance* madrasa, Clifton, Karachi.
60. Ibid.
61. Advertisement collected by the author on June 2, 2005 during a pilot survey in Karachi.
62. Riaz, volume III. A complete list of affiliated schools can also be found at AKU-EB's website, http://www.pakmed.net/college/forum/?p=2168.
63. Interview, October 8, 2007, Tuition Center, Clifton, Karachi.
64. Interview, October 8, 2007, Tuition Center, Clifton, Karachi.
65. Eickelman, *Mass Higher Education*.
66. Interview, August 29, 2007, Karachi.
67. Hirschkind, *Passional Preaching, Aural Sensibility*, 632.
68. Eickelman, Anderson, *New Media in the Muslim World*, 47.
69. Interview, July 29, 2007, Colonel Ehtesham's residence, Malir Cantonment, Karachi.
70. Interview, January 13, 2008, Read Islamic school, Defense Housing Authority, Karachi.
71. Interview, July 27, 2007, Mr. Khusro's residence, Gulshan-e-Iqbal, Karachi.
72. Jaffri, *What Really Happens inside a Madrasa*; Textbook cover of a third-grade Arabic language textbook used in an Islamic school (property of the author).

73. Herrera, *The Sanctity of the School*.
74. Riaz, volume I, July 18, 2007, Defense, Karachi.
75. Hirschkind, *Passional Preaching, Aural Sensibility*, 537.
76. Interview, July 18, 2007, Islamic school, Clifton, Karachi.
77. Interview, October 25, 2008, Quratul Ain's residence, North Nazimabad, Karachi.
78. Bourdieu, *The Forms of Capital*.
79. Leichty, *Suitably Modern*, 5.
80. Interview, August 26, 2007, Islamic school, Defense, Karachi.
81. August and November, 2007.
82. Interview, September 18, 2007, Islamic school, Gulshan-e-Iqbal, Karachi.
83. Interview, August 11, 2007, Shiite Islamic school, PECHS, Karachi.
84. Interview, January 27, 2008, Islamic school, Guru Mandir, Karachi.
85. Hoodbhoy, *Education and the State*.
86. Hefner and Zaman, *Schooling Islam*.
87. Interview, October 18, 2007, Bahadurabad, Karachi.
88. Interview, February 17, 2008, Asia's residence, Defense, Karachi.
89. Looney, *Reforming Pakistan's Educational System*, 272.
90. Interview, February 14, 2008, Jamaat-e-Islami Islamic school, Gulshan-e-Iqbal, Karachi.
91. Singer, *Pakistan's Madrassahs*.
92. Ibid.

Chapter 4

1. Altorki and El-Solh, eds., *Arab Women in the Field*.
2. Riaz, volume I.
3. Interview, October 11, 2007, MA Islamic school, Karachi.
4. October 11, 2007, MA Islamic school, Karachi.
5. Interview, MA Islamic school, February 27, 2008, Guru Mandir, Karachi.
6. Riaz, volume III, February 27, 2008, MA Islamic school, North Nazimabad.
7. Riaz, volume III, MA Islamic school, February 27, 2008.
8. Hefner and Zaman, *Schooling Islam*.
9. Asad, *Anthropology of Islam*.
10. Riaz, volume III, March 14, 2008, Deobandi Islamic school, Gulistan-e-Jauhar, Karachi.
11. Interview, March 14, 2008, Deobandi Islamic school, Gulistan-c-Jauhar, Karachi.

12. Ibid.
13. Riaz, volume III, February 1, 2008, Barelvi Islamic school, Nazimabad.
14. Ibid.
15. Riaz, volume III, February 4, 2008, Barelvi Islamic school, North Nazimabad.
16. Riaz, volume III, February 6, 2008, F. B. Area, Karachi.
17. Rahman, *Education in Pakistan*.
18. Riaz, volume II, October 22, 2007, Ahl al-Hadith Islamic school, Guru Mandir, Karachi.
19. Ibid.
20. Riaz, volume II, November 9, 2007.
21. Riaz, volume II.
22. Interview, December 15, 2007, SMA Islamic school, PECHS, Karachi.
23. Interview, January 26, 2008, SMA Islamic school, Defense, Karachi.
24. Bourdieu, *Distinction*.
25. January 26, 2008, SMA Islamic school, Defense, Karachi.
26. Riaz, volume III, January 26, 2008, SMA Islamic school, Defense, Karachi.
27. Ibid.
28. Interview, January 26, 2008, SMA Islamic school, Defense, Karachi.
29. Interview, November 7, 2007, C Islamic school, Lyari, Karachi.
30. Riaz, volume II.
31. Interview, August 22, 2007, Shiite private secular school, PECHS, Karachi.
32. Interview, November 17, 2007, Shiite Islamic school, Rizvia Society, Karachi.
33. Riaz, volume II, Shiite Islamic schools, Rizvia Society, Nazimabad and PECHS.
34. Riaz, volume II, October 8, 2007, JIMA Islamic school, Gulistan-e-Jauhar, Karachi.
35. Ibid.
36. Ibid.
37. Ibid.
38. Interview, January 20, 2008, Memon Islamic school, Memon Colony, Karachi.
39. Interview, April 29, 2008, Memon Islamic school, Memon Colony, Karachi.
40. Interview, January 20, 2008, Memon Islamic school, Memon Colony, Karachi.
41. Riaz, volume III, January 20, 2008, Memon Islamic school versus Defense area Islamic schools, Karachi.

42. Riaz, volume II, March 18, 2008, Islamic school.
43. Bourdieu, *Distinction*.

Chapter 5

1. Riaz, volume III, March 27, 2008, C1, Gulshan-e-Iqbal, Karachi.
2. Riaz, volume II, SMA Islamic school, PECHS, November 21, 2007.
3. Ibid.
4. Interview, March 11, 2008, SMA Islamic school, PECHS, Karachi.
5. Interview, August 9, 2007, JIMA Islamic school, Gulistan-e-Jauhar, Karachi.
6. Interview, April 10, 2008, C1, Gulshan-e-Iqbal, Karachi.
7. Interview, March 11, 2008, SMA Islamic school, PECHS, Karachi.
8. Riaz, volume II, September 5, 2007.
9. Ibid.
10. Interview, March 3, 2008, JIMA Islamic school, Gulistan-e-Jauhar, Karachi.
11. Riaz, volume II, August 20, 2007, JIMA Islamic school, Gulistan-e-Jauhar, Karachi.
12. Ibid.
13. Ibid.
14. Ibid.
15. Ibid.
16. Ibid.
17. Riaz, volume III, March 20, 2008, C1, Gulshan-e-Iqbal, Karachi.
18. Riaz, volume III, February 13, 2008, F. B. Area, Karachi.
19. Ibid.
20. Ibid.
21. Ibid.
22. Ibid.
23. Ali, *The Duel*.
24. Giroux, *Theory and Resistance in Education*; Malik, *Madrasas in South Asia*.
25. Eickelman, *Mass Higher Education*.
26. Interview, March 13, 2008, MA Islamic school, Nazimabad, Karachi.
27. Ibid.
28. Ibid.
29. Interview, April 2, 2008, C2, Malir Cantonment, Karachi.
30. Ibid.
31. Riaz, volume III, March 24, 2008, C1, Gulshan-e-Iqbal, Karachi.
32. Paracha, *Allah Hafiz to Khuda Hafiz*.

33. Riaz, volume II, November 12, 2007, Islamic school, Federal B Area, Karachi.
34. Ibid.
35. Riaz, volume III
36. Interview, March 20, 2008, C1, Gulshan-e-Iqbal, Karachi.
37. Willis, *Learning to Labor.*
38. Bourdieu and Passeron, *Reproduction in Education.*
39. Interview, March 27, 2008, C1, Gulshan-e-Iqbal, Karachi.
40. *Afaq Book Publisher Series.* Social studies textbook.
41. Ibid.
42. Ibid.
43. Ibid.
44. Ibid.
45. Ibid.
46. Ibid.
47. Rosser, *Contesting Historiographies in South Asia.*
48. Crompton and Stimpson, *History in Focus 1.*
49. Moss, *Oxford History for Pakistan.*
50. Crawford, *Geography for Pakistan 1.*
51. Riaz, 2010–13, Facebook correspondence.
52. Interview, April 11, 2008, C1, Gulshan-e-Iqbal, Karachi.
53. Herrera, *The Sanctity of the School.*
54. Mahmood, *Politics of Piety;* Armbrust, *Mass Culture.*
55. Interview, April 11, 2008, C1, Gulshan-e-Iqbal, Karachi.
56. Cook-Gumperz, *Social Construction of Literacy.*
57. Interview, March 26, 2008, C1, Gulshan-e-Iqbal, Karachi.
58. Interview, April 2, 2008, C2, Malir Cantonment, Karachi.
59. Ibid.
60. Interview, April 6, 2008, C1, Gulshan-e-Iqbal, Karachi.
61. Interview, August 9, 2007, Islamic school, Clifton, Karachi.
62. Interview, October 17, 2007, Islamic school, North Nazimabad, Karachi.
63. Interview, March 20, 2008, C2, Malir Cantonment, Karachi.
64. Ibid.
65. September 27, 2007, Islamic school, Malir, Karachi.
66. Riaz, volumes I–II.
67. Interview, September 27, 2007, Islamic school, Lyari, Karachi.
68. Ibid.
69. Interview, March 20, 2008, C2, Malir Cantonment, Karachi.
70. Ibid.
71. Interview, March 20, 2008, C2, Malir Cantonment, Karachi.
72. Interview, August 23, 2007, Islamic school, Gulshan-e-Iqbal, Karachi.

73. Andrabi, Das, and Khwaja, *A Dime a Day*, 344.
74. Ibid.
75. Interview, August 23, 2007, Islamic school, Gulshan-e-Iqbal, Karachi.
76. Interview, August 11, 2007, PECHS, Karachi.
77. Group interview, August 16, 2007, Islamic school, North Nazimabad, Karachi.
78. Ibid.
79. Interview, August 27, 2007, Islamic school, F. B. Area, Karachi.
80. Ibid.
81. Bourdieu and Passeron, *Reproduction in Education*.

Chapter 6

1. Starrett, *Putting Islam to Work*.
2. Willis, *Learning to Labor*.
3. Asad, *Genealogies of Religion*.
4. Herrera, *Education, Islam, and Modernity*.
5. Armbrust, *Mass Culture*.

Bibliography

Abbas, Hassan. *Pakistan's Drift into Extremism: Allah, The Army, and America's War on Terror.* Armonk: M.E. Sharpe, 2004.
Abbas, Shemeem. "The Power of English in Pakistan." *World Englishes* 12, no. 2 (1993): 147–56.
Abu-Lughod, Lila. "Zones of Theory in the Anthropology of the Arab World." *Annual Review of Anthropology* 18 (1989): 267–306.
Afaq Books Publishers. *Textbook Series.* 2008.
Ahmad, Sadaf. *Transforming Faith: The Story of Al-Huda and Islamic Revivalism among Urban Pakistani Women.* New York: Syracuse University Press, 2009.
Ali, Tariq. *The Duel: Pakistan on the Flight Path of American Power.* New York: Scribner, 2009.
Altorki, Soraya, and Camillia Fawzi El-Solh, eds. *Arab Women in the Field: Studying Your Own Society.* New York: Syracuse University Press, 1988.
Ambikar, Rucha. "Embodying the Enemy: Muslim Students in Right Wing Hindu Schools." *Anthropology News* 53, no. 7 (September 2012): 52–53. http://onlinelibrary.wiley.com/doi/10.1111/j.1556-3502.2012.53701_s.x/pdf
Anderson-Levitt, Kathryn. *Local Meanings, Global Schooling: Anthropology and World Culture Theory.* New York: Palgrave Macmillan, 2003.
Andrabi, Tahir, Jishnu Das, and Asim Ijaz Khwaja. "A Dime a Day: The Possibilities and Limits of Private Schooling in Pakistan." *Comparative Education Review* 52, no. 3 (2008): 329–355. http://www.hks.harvard.edu/fs/akhwaja/papers/PrivateSchool_CER.pdf
Anzar, Uzma. *Islamic Education: A Brief History of Madrassas with Comments on Curricula and Current Pedagogical Practices.* 2003. http://www.uvm.edu~envprog/madrassah/madrassah-history.pdf
Appadurai, Arjun. *Modernity at Large: Cultural Dimensions of Globalization.* Minneapolis: University of Minnesota Press, 1996.
Apple, Michael W. *Teachers and Texts: A Political Economy of Class and Gender Relations in Education.* New York: Routledge, 1988.
———. *Ideology and Curriculum.* New York: Routledge, 2004.

Armbrust, Walter. *Mass Culture and Modernism in Egypt*. New York: Cambridge University Press, 1996.

Asad, Talal. "The Idea of an Anthropology of Islam." In *Occasional Papers Series*, 1–22. Washington DC: Georgetown University Press, 1986.

———. *Genealogies of Religion*. Baltimore: John Hopkins University Press, 1993.

Bengelsdorf, Carollee, Margaret Cerullo, and Yogesh Chandrani, eds. *The Selected Writings of Eqbal Ahmad*. New York: Columbia University Press, 2006.

Blood, Peter R. *Pakistan: A Country Study*. Los Angeles: Claitors Publishing Division, 1995.

Bourdieu, Pierre. "The Social Space and the Genesis of Groups." *Theory and Society* 14, no. 6 (November 1985): 723–744.

———. "The Forms of Capital." In *Handbook for Theory and Research for the Sociology of Education*, edited by John G. Richardson, 241–258. New York: Greenwood, 1986.

———. *Distinction: A Social Critique of the Judgment of Taste*. Cambridge: Harvard University Press, 1987.

———, and Jean-Claude Passeron. *Reproduction in Education, Society and Culture*. London: Sage Publications, 1990.

Candland, Christopher. "Pakistan's Recent Experience in Reforming Islamic Education." In *Education Reform in Pakistan: Building for the Future*, edited by Robert M. Hathaway, 151–166. Washington DC: Woodrow Wilson International Center for Scholars Asia Program, 2005.

Cohen, Stephen Philip. *The Idea of Pakistan*. Washington DC: Brookings Institution Press, 2006.

Cook-Gumperz, Jenny. *The Social Construction of Literacy*. New York: Cambridge University Press, 2006.

Constitution of the Islamic Republic of Pakistan. *Article 251*. Government of Pakistan, 1973. http://www.pakistani.org/pakistan/constitution/part12.ch4.html

Crawford, Doreen. *Geography for Pakistan 1*. Malaysia: Peak Publishing, 2008.

Crick, R. M. "Anthropology of Knowledge." *Annual Review of Anthropology* 11 (October 1982): 287–313.

Crompton, and Stimpson. *History in Focus 1*. Malaysia: Peak Publishing, 2004.

Dance, L. Janelle. *Tough Fronts: The Impact of Street Culture on Schooling*. New York: Routledge, 2002.

Dhofier, Zamakhsyari. *The Pesantren Tradition: The Role of the Kyai in the Maintenance of Traditional Islam in Java*. Tempe: Arizona State University Press, 1999.

Dixson, Adrienne D., and Celia K. Rousseau. *Critical Race Theory in Education: All God's Children Got a Song*. New York: Routledge, 2006.

Eickelman, Dale F. "Mass Higher Education and the Religious Imagination in Arab Societies." *American Ethnologist* 19, no. 4 (1992): 643–655.

———, and Jon W. Anderson, eds. *New Media in the Muslim World: The Emerging Public Sphere.* Bloomington: Indiana University Press, 2003.

Esposito, John L. *Unholy War: Terror in the Name of Islam.* New York: Oxford University Press, 2003.

———. *The Islamic Threat: Myth or Reality?* New York: Oxford University Press, 1999.

Giroux, Henry A. *Theory and Resistance in Education: Towards a Pedagogy for the Opposition.* Westport: Bergin and Garvey, 2001.

Government of Pakistan. *National Education Policy.* Islamabad: Ministry of Education, 1959.

———. *National Education Policy.* Islamabad: Ministry of Education, 1979.

———. *Deeni Madaris ki Jame Report [Urdu].* Islamabad: Islamic Education Research Cell, Ministry of Education, Government of Pakistan, 1988.

———. *National Education Policy 1992–2002.* Islamabad: Ministry of Education, 1992.

———. *National Education Policy 1998–2010.* Islamabad: Ministry of Education, 1998.

Haj, Samira. *Reconfiguring Islamic Tradition: Reform, Rationality, and Modernity.* Palo Alto: Stanford University Press, 2008.

Haqqani, Husain. "The Role of Islam in Pakistan's Future." *The Washington Quarterly* 28, no. 1 (2004): 83–96.

———. *Pakistan: Between Mosque and Military.* Washington DC: Carnegie Endowment for International Peace, 2005.

Hefner, Robert W., and Mohammad Qasim Zaman, eds. *Schooling Islam: The Culture and Politics of Modern Muslim Education.* Princeton: Princeton University Press, 2007.

Herrera, Linda Ann. *The Sanctity of the School: New Islamic Education and Modern Egypt.* PhD Dissertation, Columbia University, 2000.

———. "Education, Islam, and Modernity: Beyond Westernization and Centralization." *Comparative Education Review* 48, no. 3 (2004): 318–326.

Hirschkind, Charles. "Passional Preaching, Aural Sensibility, and the Islamic Revival." In *A Reader in the Anthropology of Religion*, edited by Michael Lambek, 544–559. Malden: Blackwell Publishers, 2002.

Hoodbhoy, Pervez. *Education and the State: Fifty Years of Pakistan.* New York: Oxford University Press, 1998.

Human Rights Commission of Pakistan Report. *The Education Budget in Pakistan.* Islamabad: Human Rights Commission of Pakistan, 2004. http://www.commonwealtheducationfund.org/downloads/Pakistan%20Financing%20of%20Education.pdf

Hussain, Fayyaz. *An Ethnographic Study of Jamia Ashrafia: A Religious School at Lahore with Special Emphasis on Socio-Practical Relevance of Its Objective.* M.Sc Dissertation. Department of Anthropology. Quaid-e-Azam University, Islamabad, 1994.

Hussain, Zahid. *Frontline Pakistan: The Struggle with Militant Islam.* New York: Columbia University Press, 2007.

International Crisis Group. "Pakistan: Madrassas. Extremism and the Military." *International Advisory Group Asia Report* 36. July 29. Islamabad, 2002.

———. *Pakistan: The Mullah and the Military.* Islamabad: International Crisis Group, 2003.

IPS Task Force Report. *Pakistan Religious Education Institutions: An Overview.* Islamabad: Institute of Policy Studies, 2002.

Jeffrelot, Christophe. *A History of Pakistan and Its Origins.* London: Anthem Press, 2004.

Jaffri, Farhan. "What Really Happens Inside a Madrasa. Express Tribune Blog," December 10, 2011. http://blogs.tribune.com.pk/story/8983/what-really-happens-inside-a-madrassa/

Jones, Owen Bennett. *Pakistan: Eye of the Storm.* New Haven: Yale University Press, 2003.

Kaplan, Robert D. *Soldiers of God: With Islamic Warriors in Afghanistan and Pakistan.* New York: Vintage, 2001.

Kepel, Gilles. *Jihad: The Trail of Political Islam.* Cambridge, Massachusetts: The Belknap Press of Harvard University Press, 2002.

Khan, Shahrukh Rafi. *Basic Education in Rural Pakistan: A Comparative Institutional Analysis of Government, Private and NGO Schools.* Karachi: Oxford University Press, 2006.

Kondo, Dorinne K. *Crafting Selves: Power, Gender, and Discourses of Identity in a Japanese Workplace.* Chicago: University Of Chicago Press, 1990.

Levinson, Bradley. "Resituating the Place of Educational Discourse in Anthropology." *American Anthropologist* 101, no. 3 (1999): 594–604.

Liechty, Mark. *Suitably Modern: Making Middle-Class Culture in a New Consumer Society.* Princeton: Princeton University Press, 2003.

Liow, Joseph Chinyong. "The Challenge of Islamic Reformism." In *Islam, Education, and Reform in Southern Thailand: Tradition and Transformation*, 76–99. Singapore: Institute of Southeast Asian Studies, 2010.

Lodhi, A. 2007. "Mosque-Schools to Be Merged with Government Primary Schools." *Daily Times*, July 25, 2007. Retrieved from http://www.dailytimes.com.pk/default.asp?page=2007%5C07%5C25%5Cstory_25-7-2007_pg7_32

Looney, Robert. "Reforming Pakistan's Educational System: The Challenge of the Madrassas." *The Journal of Social, Political, and Economic Studies* 28, no. 3 (2003): 257–274.

Lyon, Stephen, Iain R. Edgar, and Ali Khan, eds. *Shaping a Nation: An Examination of Education in Pakistan*. Karachi: Oxford University Press, 2010.
Macleod, Arlene Elowe. *Accommodating Protest: Working Women, the New Veiling, and Change in Cairo*. Cairo: American University in Cairo Press, 1992.
Mahmood, Saba. *Politics of Piety: The Islamic Revival and the Feminist Subject*. Princeton: Princeton University Press, 2004.
Malik, Jamal. *Colonialization of Islam: Dissolution of Traditional Institutions in Pakistan*. Lahore: Vanguard Books, 1996.
———. *Madrasas in South Asia: Teaching Terror?* New York: Routledge, 2008.
Masud, Muḥammad Khalid. "Communicative Action and the Social Construction of Sharia in Pakistan." In *Religion, Social Practice, and Contested Hegemonies: Reconstructing the Public Sphere in Muslim Majority Societies*, edited by Armando Salvatore and Mark Le Vine, 155–179. New York: Palgrave Macmillan, 2005.
Moss, Peter. *Oxford History for Pakistan: Book 1*. Karachi: Oxford University Press, 1997.
Narayan, Kirin. "How Native Is a 'Native' Anthropologist?" *American Anthropologist* 95, no. 3 (1993): 671–686.
Nawaz, Muḥammad. *Islam and Muslim Psyche: Reason, Modernity and Orthodoxy*. Bloomington: AuthorHouse, 2008.
Ogbu J. *The Next Generation: An Ethnography of Education in an Urban Neighborhood*. New York: Academic Press, 1974.
Ochs, E. "Clarification and Culture." In *Meaning, Form, and Use in Context: Linguistic Applications*, edited by D. Schiffrin, 325–341. Washington DC: Georgetown University Press, 1984.
Ostrove, Joan M., and Elizabeth R. Cole, eds. "Privileging Class: Toward a Critical Psychology of Social Class in the Context of Education." *Journal of Social Issues* 59, no. 4 (2003): 677–692.
Ouis, Pernilla. *Power, Person, and Place: Tradition, Modernity, and Environment in the United Arab Emirates*. Sweden: Lund University, 2002.
Paracha, Nadeem F. "Allah Hafiz to Khuda Hafiz." *Dawn* newspaper, Pakistan, May 24, 2009. http://progressivescottishmuslims.blogspot.com/2010/06/allah-hafiz-to-khuda-hafiz.html
Popkewitz, T., & Fendler, Lynn, eds. *Critical Theories in Education: Changing Terrains of Knowledge and Politics*. New York: Routledge, 1999.
Qadeer, Mohammad A. *Pakistan: Social and Cultural Transformation*. New York: Routledge, 2006.
Raza, Rafi. *Zulfikar Ali Bhutto and Pakistan 1967–1977*. Karachi: Oxford University Press, 1997.
Reed-Danahey, Deborah. *Education and Identity in Rural France: The Politics of Schooling*. New York: Cambridge University Press, 2004.

Rahman, Tariq. "Language, Religion and Identity in Pakistan: Language-Teaching in Pakistan Madrassas." *Ethnic Studies Report* 16, no. 2 (1998): 197–214.

———. *Denizens of Alien Worlds: A Study of Education, Inequality and Polarization in Pakistan.* Karachi: Oxford University Press, 2005.

———. "Education in Pakistan: A Survey." In *Pakistan on the Brink: Politics, Economics, and Society*, edited by Craig Baxter, 171–190. Lanham: Lexington Books, 2004.

Riaz, Sanaa. Field notes. Volumes I–III, 2004–08. Karachi, Pakistan.

Riaz, Sanaa. Notes compiled through Islamic schools' group pages and personal interaction on Facebook, 2010–13.

Rosser, Y. C. "Contesting Historiographies in South Asia: The Islamization of Pakistani Social Studies Textbooks." In *Religious Fundamentalism in the Contemporary World*, edited by S. C. Saha, 265–307. Lanham: Lexington Books, 2004.

Roy, Olivier. *Secularism Confronts Islam.* New York: Columbia University Press, 2007.

Said, Edward. *Orientalism.* New York: Vintage, 1979.

Sikand, Yoginder. *Bastions of the Believers: Madrasas and Islamic Education in India.* New York: Penguin Global, 2006.

Singer, P. W. *Pakistan's Madrassahs: Ensuring a System of Education Not Jihad.* Washington: Brookings Institution, 2001. http://www.brookings.edu/papers/2001/11pakistan_singer.aspx

Sivan, Emmanuel. *Radical Islam: Medieval Theology and Modern Politics.* New Haven: Yale University Press, 1990.

Spindler, George Dearborn, ed. *Education and Cultural Process: Anthropological Approaches.* Long Grove. Waveland Press, 1997.

Srinivas, Mysore Narasimhachar. *The Remembered Village.* Berkeley: University of California Press, 1976.

Starrett, Gregory. *Putting Islam to Work.* Berkeley: University of California Press, 1998.

Stern, Jessica. *Terror in the Name of God.* New York: Harper Perennial, 2004.

Tambiah, Stanley J. *Leveling Crowds: Ethnonationalist Conflicts and Collective Violence in South Asia.* Berkeley: University of California Press, 1997.

Wafaqul Madaris Al-Arabiyya. *Wafaqul Madaris Al-Arabiyya Monthly Magazine.* Multan: Wafaqul Madaris Al-Arabiyya, February 2008. [In Urdu]

———. *Wafaqul Madaris Al-Arabiyya Monthly Magazine.* Multan: Wafaqul Madaris Al-Arabiyya, May 2007. [In Urdu]

Willis, Paul. *Learning to Labor.* New York: Columbia University Press, 1981.

Zeghal, Malika. "Religion and Politics in Egypt: The Ulema of Al-Azhar, Radical Islam and the State (1952–94)." *International Journal of Middle East Studies* 31, no. 3 (1999): 371–399.

Glossary

Terms	Meanings
Abaya	Cloak worn by some Muslim women
Adl	Justice
Ahle-Tashi	Followers of Twelver Shiism
Ahl al-Hadith	A Sunni subsect that emphasizes the use to understand Islamic injunctions
Aqaid	Theology
Aqaid-e-Islam	Islamic beliefs
Aql	Knowledge
Alim	Islamic scholar. Also, middle to high level in madrasa education
Alima	Female Islamic scholar
Alimat	Female Islamic scholars. Plural of Alima
Allah hafiz	Arabized version of Khuda hafiz, good bye
A-level	Grades 11 and 12. Equivalent to intermediate of the national education system
Assalamoaleikum	Greeting, literally, peace be upon you
Ashura	Tenth day of Muharram in the Islamic calendar believed to be the day Prophet Muhammad's grandson Husayn, family and supporters were tragically killed in the Battle of Karbala
Ayat	Verses of the Quran
Bashar	Mortal
Bida	Innovations in Islamic practice considered equal to sin
Bismillah	In the name of God (said before beginning any work or action to bless it)
Dakhil	Primary level in madrasa education
Dawa	Islamic proselytization

Deobandi	A Sunni subsect that believes in following the religious experts who laid down the four schools of thought in Islamic jurisprudence
Din	Religion
Durood	Phrase(s) recited in praise of Prophet Muhammad
Dunya	World. Sometimes used as the opposite of din (religion)
Farooqi	People who claim ancestry from Umar ibn al-Khattab, the second caliph of Islam
Fazil	Higher secondary level in madrasa education
Fiqh	Islamic jurisprudence
Hadith	Reports on the sayings and actions of Prophet Muhammad
Hamd	Poetry sung in praise of Allah
Hazrat	Honorific manner of addressing a holy or spiritual person
Hifz	Quranic memorization
Hafiz/Hafiz al-Quran	One who memorizes the Quran
Huffaz/Huffaz al-Quran	People who memorize the Quran. Plural of Hafiz
Huququl-ibad	Honoring the rights of other human beings
Ilm	Knowledge
Imam	Islamic leader. Also refers to the series of seven (in Ismaili Shiism) or twelve leaders (in Twelver/Ithna Ashari Shiism) who were descendants in the line of Prophet Muhammad
Iman	Faith
Inshallah	God willing
Islami	Islamic
Islamiat	Islamic studies. Compulsory subject from primary to undergraduate level in public schools, colleges, and universities
Ithna Ashari/Twelver	Member of the Shiite majority sub-sect that believes in twelve divine leaders, imams, the first being Muhammed's son-in-law Ali, who could not ascend to the Caliphate. The twelfth imam is in occultation. Also see Imam
Jahiliyya	Described in Islamic history as the period of ignorance and darkness that preceded Islam
Jamaats/jamaat khanas	Memon Pakistanis' congregation sites or centers
Jamaat Ahle Sunnat	The religious organization representing Barelvi Sunni Muslims

Jamaat-e-Islami	An Islamic political party in Pakistan founded by Abul Ala Maududi in British India
Jazak Allah	All praise belongs to Allah
Jihad	War in the defense of Islam by arms, conduct, and words
Jihadi	Mujahid or one who fights against the infidels on the battlefield
Kalima	Six compilations of Quranic verses that Muslims memorize
Kamil	College and post-graduate level in madrasa education
Khuda hafiz	Good-bye
Madhab	Sect or one of the four schools of thought in Islamic jurisprudence
Madrasas	Religious seminaries
Majlis	Shiite gathering to remember Ali and other members of Prophet Muhammad's family
Marsiya	Elegiac poetry to commemorate Husayn ibn Ali, Prophet Muhammad's grandson, martyred in the Battle of Karbala
Mashallah	All praise goes to Allah/nothing happens without god's will
Maslak	Sect or one of the four schools of thought in Islamic jurisprudence. Used synonymous to madhab
Muezzin	The person at the mosque who calls Muslim to prayers
Mufti	Sunni scholar who interprets Islamic jurisprudence
Muharram	The first and one of the four holiest months in Islamic calendar
Mullah/maulvi	Muslim man educated in Islamic theology. Sometimes used for a group of religious men. Often used humorously for a person who becomes religious
Mullani	Muslim woman educated in Islamic theology. Sometimes used for a group of religious men. Often used humorously for a person who becomes religious
Murgha	Rooster
Naat	Poetry sung in the praise of Prophet Muhammad
Nazira	Quranic reading with correct pronunciation of words and accents

Nauzubillah	Literally, we seek refuge in Allah from evil Said before saying something negative about Islam or Islamic holy figures
Nikah	Islamic marriage
Nur	Spiritual or divine light
Pir	Guide or master in Sufism
Qirat	Quranic recitation
Qari	One who (professionally) recites the Quran
Qul	Last four chapters of the Quran beginning with the word qul/Say
Rasul Allah	Literally, Prophet of Allah. Muhmmad
Sanad	Degree granted by a madrasa in Pakistan equivalent to a Master's degree from a secular institution
Sharia	Divine law in Islam
Sirat rasul Allah	Life of Prophet Muhammad that stands as a source on information in addition to Quran and Hadith
Sabah al-khayr	Good morning in Arabic
Sadqa-e-jaaria	Sacrifice in the name of humanity
Sawaab	Divine blessing or reward in Islam
Sayyid	People who claim direct descendency from Prophet Muhammad
Subhanallah	God be to glorious
Subh bakhayr	Good morning in Urdu
Sunna	Words and actions of Prophet Muhammad
Surat/Sura	Quranic chapter
Surat al-Baqara	The second and longest chapter of the Quran
Tafsir	Quranic exegesis
Tajwid	Quranic elocution
Tawhid	Islamic belief in the oneness of god
Ulema	Muslim scholars. Plural of Alim
Umma	The community of Muslims believers across the world
Uswa hasana	The good example of Prophet Muhammad
Waqf (plural: awqaf)	Charitable endowment from the state to madrasas
Wudu	Ablution before prayers
Yom-e-Husayn	Commemoration of the death anniversary of Imam Husayn, Prophet Muhammad's grandson tragically killed in the Battle of Karbala
Zakat	Islamic tax liable on all Muslims
Zuhr	Second, mid-day prayer for Muslims

Index

Ahl al-Hadith
  Islamic schools, 95–96

Barelvi
  Deobandi versus, 90–92
  Islamic schools, 93–96
Bhutto, Benazir, 55
Bhutto's Islamic socialism, 63

class
  elevation through Islamic education, 24, 46, 79, 99, 110, 163, 164
  Islamic education and, 27, 28, 42–47, 76–84, 162–163
  Islamic practice and, 45
  Islamic school pedagogies and, 146–150

Deobandi, 27, 28
  Islamic schools, 90–93
  see also Jamaat-e-Islami

education in Pakistan, 49–50, 59, 60–62
  Aga Khan Board, reform in, 68, 69
  private secular schools, 56, 57
  public schools, 50, 51
  school subjects, 59
  state policies on, 55, 60–62
  tuition culture in, 69, 70
  see also O-level and Matric system; Islamic education in Pakistan; Islamization

Islam
  definition, 29
  Islamiat, 59, 60, 61, 101, 102
    Aga Khan Board curriculum for, 68, 69
    Islamic school, 33, 34, 35, 41, 91–94, 97, 123–130, 135–137
    textbooks of, 138, 139
  Islamic education in Pakistan, 17, 40, 41
    colonization of traditional, 33
    digitization of, 70–72
    mosque-schools, 54–55
    see also Islamic schools; madrasas; Western education
  Islamic Enlightenment, 28
    Western enlightenment and, 35
    see also Islamic modernity

Islamic modernity
  Objectification of religion, 34
  Western modernity, versus, 32, 36
  see also secularization
Islamic school global prototypes
  Bangladeshi, 47
  Egyptian, 17–20
  Indian, 20–26
  Indonesian, 14, 15
  Thai, 15–17
Islamic schools
  as agency, 163
  functionalization of, 41, 42
  Islamic appearance in, 119
  modernization of, 42
  morning assembly in, 121, 122
  prayer in, 122, 123
  reasons for emergence of, 42, 62–65, 72–75
  subjects taught at, 85
Islamic tradition, 29, 27, 30
  Islamic tradition, versus, 31
  just Islam, 30–31
Islamization
  as compatibility, 30
  curriculum de-Islamization, 142, 144
  jihad and, 63
  of curriculum, 59, 60, 64, 142, 143
  state and, 36, 63, 64
  see also Mullah-military alliance

Jamaat-e-Islami, 5, 6, 21, 65
  Islamic schools of, 22, 104, 105

linguistic/communal Islamic schools, 105–108

Madrasas, 51–54, 66–68
Maududi, 21, 22, 104
  see also Jamaat-e-Islami
Montessori
  Islamic school, 114–118
Mullah-military alliance, 2, 33
Musharraf's Enlightened Moderation, 64, 65

Nawaz Sharif, 55

O-level and Matric system, 57–59, 68, 69

secularization, 28, 35, 36
Shiite Islamic schools
  commercial Shiite, 101–103
  madrasa-alumni operated, 97, 98
  Saturday type of, 98–100
subjectivities in Islamic schools
  class, 146–149
  gender, 37–40, 108–110
  Islamic, 114–138, 144–146
  Islamic subjectivities through textbooks, 138–142
  national subjectivities through textbooks, 144–146
  secular subjectivities through textbooks, 142–144
Sunni Islamic schools

commercial Sunni, 101
madrasa-alumni operated, 88–90

Western education, 44

Zia-ul-Haq, 36, 63, 64
see also Islamization
Zoroastrian religious schools, 110, 111

GPSR Compliance

The European Union's (EU) General Product Safety Regulation (GPSR) is a set of rules that requires consumer products to be safe and our obligations to ensure this.

If you have any concerns about our products, you can contact us on

ProductSafety@springernature.com

In case Publisher is established outside the EU, the EU authorized representative is:

Springer Nature Customer Service Center GmbH
Europaplatz 3
69115 Heidelberg, Germany

www.ingramcontent.com/pod-product-compliance
Lightning Source LLC
LaVergne TN
LVHW051912060526
838200LV00004B/100